THE EDUCATION OF
HYMAN KAPLAN

For Pearl Rosenthal Leo Rosten
with thanks —

THE
EDUCATION OF
HYMAN KAPLAN

BY LEONARD Q. ROSS

HBMC

Harcourt, Brace & World, Inc., New York

To My Mother and Father

ACKNOWLEDGMENTS

I wish to express my gratitude to the Editors of *The New Yorker*, in which these stories first appeared, for the excellence of their criticism and for their encouragement throughout; to my sister, Helen, for many valuable suggestions; and to my wife, for her insights as a first reader, her labors in preparing the manuscript for publication, and her patience during those extraordinary hours when Mr. Kaplan tyrannized our lives.

L. Q. R.

CONTENTS

THE EDUCATION OF
HYMAN KAPLAN

THE RATHER
DIFFICULT CASE
OF MR. K*A*P*L*A*N

IN the third week of the new term, Mr. Parkhill was forced to the conclusion that Mr. Kaplan's case was rather difficult. Mr. Kaplan first came to his special attention, out of the thirty-odd adults in the beginners' grade of the American Night Preparatory School for Adults ("English—Americanization—Civics—Preparation for Naturalization"), through an exercise the class had submitted. The exercise was entitled "Fifteen Common Nouns and Their Plural Forms." Mr. Parkhill came to one paper which included the following:

house .... makes.......... houses
dog ....   "   .... dogies
libary ....   "   .... Public libary
cat ....   "   .... Katz

Mr. Parkhill read this over several times, very thoughtfully. He decided that here was a student who might, unchecked, develop into a "problem case." It was clearly a case that called for special attention. He turned the page over and read the name. It was printed in large, firm letters with red crayon. Each letter was outlined in blue. Between every two letters was a star, carefully drawn, in green. The multi-colored whole spelled, unmistakably, H * Y * M * A * N K * A * P * L * A * N.

This Mr. Kaplan was in his forties, a plump, red-faced gentleman, with wavy blond hair, *two* fountain pens in his outer pocket, and a perpetual smile. It was a strange smile, Mr. Parkhill remarked: vague, bland, and consistent in its monotony. The thing that emphasized it for Mr. Parkhill was that it never seemed to leave the face of Mr. Kaplan, even during Recitation and Speech period. This disturbed Mr. Parkhill considerably, because Mr. Kaplan was particularly bad in Recitation and Speech.

Mr. Parkhill decided he had not applied himself as conscientiously as he might to Mr. Kaplan's case. That very night he called on Mr. Kaplan first.

"Won't *you* take advantage of Recitation and Speech practice, Mr. Kaplan?" he asked, with an encouraging smile.

Mr. Kaplan smiled back and answered promptly, "Vell, I'll tell abot Prazidents United States. Fife

Prazidents United States is Abram Lincohen, he vas freeink de neegers; Hodding, Coolitch, Judge Vashington, an' Banjamin Frenklin."

Further encouragement revealed that in Mr. Kaplan's literary Valhalla the "most famous tree American wriders" were Jeck Laundon, Valt Viterman, and the author of "Hawk L. Barry-Feen," one Mocktvain. Mr. Kaplan took pains to point out that he did not mention Relfvaldo Amerson because "He is a poyet, an' I'm talkink abot wriders."

Mr. Parkhill diagnosed the case as one of "inability to distinguish between 'a' and 'e.' " He concluded that Mr. Kaplan *would* need special attention. He was, frankly, a little disturbed.

Mr. Kaplan's English showed no improvement during the next hard weeks. The originality of his spelling and pronunciation, however, flourished— like a sturdy flower in the good, rich earth. A man to whom "Katz" is the plural of "cat" soon soars into higher and more ambitious endeavor. As a one-paragraph "Exercise in Composition," Mr. Kaplan submitted:

When people is meating on the boulvard, on going away one is saying, "I am glad I mat you," and the other is giving answer, "Mutual."

Mr. Parkhill felt that perhaps Mr. Kaplan had overreached himself, and should be confined to the simpler exercises.

Mr. Kaplan was an earnest student. He worked hard, knit his brows regularly (albeit with that smile), did all his homework, and never missed a class. Only once did Mr. Parkhill feel that Mr. Kaplan might, perhaps, be a little more *serious* about his work. That was when he asked Mr. Kaplan to "give a noun."

"Door," said Mr. Kaplan, smiling.

It seemed to Mr. Parkhill that "door" had been given only a moment earlier, by Miss Mitnick.

"Y-es," said Mr. Parkhill. "Er—and another noun?"

"Another door," Mr. Kaplan replied promptly.

Mr. Parkhill put him down as a doubtful "C." Everything pointed to the fact that Mr. Kaplan might have to be kept on an extra three months before he was ready for promotion to Composition, Grammar, and Civics, with Miss Higby.

One night Mrs. Moskowitz read a sentence, from "English for Beginners," in which "the vast deserts of America" were referred to. Mr. Parkhill soon discovered that poor Mrs. Moskowitz did not know the meaning of "vast." "Who can tell us the meaning of 'vast'?" asked Mr. Parkhill lightly.

Mr. Kaplan's hand shot up, volunteering wisdom. He was all proud grins. Mr. Parkhill, in the rashness of the moment, nodded to him.

Mr. Kaplan rose, radiant with joy. " 'Vast!' It's commink fromm *diraction*. Ve have four diractions: de naut, de sot, de heast, and de vast."

Mr. Parkhill shook his head. "Er—that is 'west,' Mr. Kaplan." He wrote "VAST" and "WEST" on the blackboard. To the class he added, tolerantly, that Mr. Kaplan was apparently thinking of "west," whereas it was "vast" which was under discussion.

This seemed to bring a great light into Mr. Kaplan's inner world. "So is 'vast' vat you eskink?"

Mr. Parkhill admitted that it was "vast" for which he was asking.

"Aha!" cried Mr. Kaplan. "You minn '*vast*,' not" —with scorn—" 'vast.' "

"Yes," said Mr. Parkhill, faintly.

"Hau Kay!" said Mr. Kaplan, essaying the vernacular. "Ven I'm buyink a suit clothes, I'm gattink de cawt, de pents, an' de vast!"

Stunned, Mr. Parkhill shook his head, very sadly.

"I'm afraid that you've used still another word, Mr. Kaplan."

Oddly enough, this seemed to give Mr. Kaplan great pleasure.

Several nights later Mr. Kaplan took advantage of Open Questions period. This ten-minute period was Mr. Parkhill's special innovation in the American Night Preparatory School for Adults. It was devoted to answering any questions which the students might care to raise about any difficulties which they might have encountered during the course of their adventures with the language. Mr. Parkhill enjoyed Open Questions. He liked to clear up *practical* problems. He felt he was being ever so much more constructive that way. Miss Higby had once told him that he was a born Open Questions teacher.

"Plizz, Mr. Pockheel," asked Mr. Kaplan as soon as the period opened. "Vat's de minnink fromm—" It sounded, in Mr. Kaplan's rendition, like "a big department."

" 'A big department,' Mr. Kaplan?" asked Mr. Parkhill, to make sure.

"Yassir!" Mr. Kaplan's smile was beauteous to behold. "In de stritt, ven I'm valkink, I'm hearink like 'I big de pottment.' "

It was definitely a pedagogical opportunity.

"Well, class," Mr. Parkhill began. "I'm sure that you have all—"

He told them that they had all probably done some shopping in the large downtown stores. (Mr. Kaplan nodded.) In these large stores, he said, if they wanted to buy a pair of shoes, for example, they went to a special *part* of the store, where only shoes were sold—a *shoe* department. (Mr. Kaplan nodded.) If they wanted a table, they went to a different *part* of the store, where *tables* were sold. (Mr. Kaplan nodded.) If they wanted to buy, say, a goldfish, they went to still another part of the store, where gold-fish . . . (Mr. Kaplan frowned; it was clear that Mr. Kaplan had never bought a goldfish.)

"Well, then," Mr. Parkhill summed up hastily, "each article is sold in a different *place*. These different and special places are called *departments*." He printed "D-E-P-A-R-T-M-E-N-T" on the board in large, clear capitals. "And a *big* department, Mr. Kaplan, is merely such a department which is large —*big!*"

He put the chalk down and wiped his fingers.

"Is that clear now, class?" he asked, with a little smile. (It was rather an ingenious explanation, he

thought; it might be worth repeating to Miss Higby
during the recess.)

It *was* clear. There were thirty nods of approval.
But Mr. Kaplan looked uncertain. It was obvious that
Mr. Kaplan, a man who would not compromise with
truth, did *not* find it clear.

"Isn't that clear *now*, Mr. Kaplan?" asked Mr.
Parkhill anxiously.

Mr. Kaplan pursed his lips in thought. "It's a *fine*
haxplination, Titcher," he said generously, "but I
don' unnistand vy I'm hearink de voids de vay I do.
Simms to me it's used in annodder minnink."

"There's really only one meaning for 'a big department.' " Mr. Parkhill was definitely worried by
this time. "*If* that's the phrase you mean."

Mr. Kaplan nodded gravely. "Oh, dat's de phrase
—ufcawss! It sonds like dat—or maybe a leetle more
like '*I* big de pottment.' "

Mr. Parkhill took up the chalk. ("*I* big department" was obviously a case of Mr. Kaplan's own
curious audition.) He repeated the explanation carefully, this time embellishing the illustrations with a
shirt department, a victrola section, and "a separate
part of the store where, for example, you buy canaries,
or other birds."

Mr. Kaplan sat entranced. He followed it all politely, even the part about "canaries, or other birds." He smiled throughout with consummate re-assurance.

Mr. Parkhill was relieved, assuming, in his folly, that Mr. Kaplan's smiles were a testimony to his exposition. But when he had finished, Mr. Kaplan shook his head once more, this time with a new and superior firmness.

"Is the explanation *still* not clear?" Mr. Parkhill was genuinely concerned by this time.

"Is de haxplination clear!" cried Mr. Kaplan with enthusiasm. "Ha! I should live so! Soitinly! Clear like *gold!* So clear! An' netcheral too! But Mr. Pockhecl—"

"Go on, Mr. Kaplan," said Mr. Parkhill, studying the white dust on his fingers. There was, after all, nothing more to be done.

"Vell! I tink it's more like '*I* big de pottment.' "

"Go on, Mr. Kaplan, go on." (*Domine, dirige nos.*)

Mr. Kaplan rose. His smile was broad, luminous, transcendent; his manner was regal.

"I'm hearink it in de stritt. Somtimes I'm stendink in de stritt, talkink to a frand, or mine vife, mine brodder—or maybe only stendink. An' somvun is pessink arond me. An' by hexident he's givink me a bump, you know, a *poosh!* Vell, he says, 'Axcuse me!' no? But somtimes, an' *dis* is vat I minn, he's sayink, '*I big de pottment!*' "

Mr. Parkhill studied the picture of "Abram Lincohen" on the back wall, as if reluctant to face reality. He wondered whether he could reconcile it with his conscience if he were to promote Mr. Kaplan to Composition, Grammar, and Civics—at once. Another three months of Recitation and Speech might, after all, be nothing but a waste of Mr. Kaplan's valuable time.

MR. K*A*P*L*A*N,
THE COMPARATIVE,
AND THE SUPERLATIVE

FOR two weeks Mr. Parkhill had been delaying the inescapable: Mr. Kaplan, like the other students in the beginners' grade of the American Night Preparatory School for Adults, would have to present a composition for class analysis. All the students had had their turn writing the assignment on the board, a composition of one hundred words, entitled "My Job." Now only Mr. Kaplan's rendition remained.

It would be more accurate to say Mr. K * A * P-L * A * N's rendition of the assignment remained, for even in thinking of that distinguished student, Mr. Parkhill saw the image of his unmistakable signature, in all its red-blue-green glory. The multicolored characters were more than a trademark; they were an assertion of individuality, a symbol of singularity, a proud expression of Mr. Kaplan's Inner Self. To Mr. Parkhill, the signature took on added meaning because it was associated with the man who had said his youthful ambition had been to become "a phy-

sician and sergeant," the Titan who had declined
the verb "to fail": "fail, failed, bankropt."

One night, after the two weeks' procrastination,
Mr. Parkhill decided to face the worst. "Mr. Kaplan,
I think it's your turn to—er—write your composition
on the board."

Mr. Kaplan's great, buoyant smile grew more
great and more buoyant. "My!" he exclaimed. He
rose, looked around at the class proudly as if sur-
veying the blessed who were to witness a linguistic
tour de force, stumbled over Mrs. Moskowitz's feet
with a polite "Vould you be so kindly?" and took his
place at the blackboard. There he rejected several
pieces of chalk critically, nodded to Mr. Parkhill—
it was a nod of distinct reassurance—and then printed
in firm letters:

> My Job A Cotter In Dress Faktory
>   Comp. by
> H * Y *

"You need not write your name on the board,"
interrupted Mr. Parkhill quickly. "Er—to save
time . . ."

Mr. Kaplan's face expressed astonishment. "Podden me, Mr. Pockheel. But de name is by me *pot* of mine composition."

"Your name is *part* of the composition?" asked Mr. Parkhill in an anxious tone.

"Yas*sir!*" said Mr. Kaplan with dignity. He printed the rest of H * Y * M * A * N K * A * P-L * A * N for all to see and admire. You could tell it was a disappointment for him not to have colored chalk for this performance. In pale white the elegance of his work was dissipated. The name, indeed, seemed unreal, the letters stark, anemic, almost denuded.

His brow wrinkled and perspiring, Mr. Kaplan wrote the saga of A Cotter In Dress Faktory on the board, with much scratching of the chalk and an undertone of sound. Mr. Kaplan repeated each word to himself softly, as if trying to give to its spelling some of the flavor and originality of his pronunciation. The smile on the face of Mr. Kaplan had taken on something beatific and imperishable: it was his first experience at the blackboard; it was his moment of glory. He seemed to be writing more slowly than necessary as if to prolong the ecstasy of his Hour. When he had finished he said "Hau Kay" with dis-

tinct regret in his voice, and sat down. Mr. Parkhill
observed the composition in all its strange beauty:

My Job A Cotter In Dress Faktory

Comp. by

H * Y * M * A * N   K * A * P * L * A * N

Shakspere is saying what fulls man is and I am feeling just the same way when I am thinking about mine
job a cotter in Dress Faktory on 38 st. by 7 av. For
why should we slafing in dark place by laktric lights
and all kinds hot for $30 or maybe $36 with overtime,
for Boss who is fat and driving in fency automobil?
I ask! Because we are the deprassed workers of world.
And are being exployted. By Bosses. In mine shop is
no difference. Oh how bad is laktric light, oh how is
all kinds hot. And when I am telling Foreman should
be better conditions he hollers, Kaplan you redical!!

At this point a glazed look came into Mr. Parkhill's eyes, but he read on.

So I keep still and work by bad light and always hot.
But somday will the workers making Bosses to work!
And then Kaplan will give to them bad laktric and positively no windows for the air should come in! So they
can know what it means to slafe! Kaplan will make

Foreman a cotter like he is. And give the most bad
dezigns to cot out. Justice.

Mine job is cotting Dress dezigns.

T-H-E   E-N-D

Mr. Parkhill read the amazing document over
again. His eyes, glazed but a moment before, were
haunted now. It was true: spelling, diction, sentence
structure, punctuation, capitalization, the use of the
present perfect for the present—all true.

"Is planty mistakes, I s'pose," suggested Mr. Kaplan modestly.

"Y-yes . . . yes, there are many mistakes."

"Dat's because I'm tryink to give *dip ideas*," said
Mr. Kaplan with the sigh of those who storm heaven.

Mr. Parkhill girded his mental loins. "Mr. Kaplan—er—your composition doesn't really meet the
assignment. You haven't described your *job*, what
you *do*, what your work *is*."

"Vell, it's not soch a interastink jop," said Mr.
Kaplan.

"Your composition is not a simple exposition. It's
more of a—well, an *essay* on your *attitude*."

"Oh, fine!" cried Mr. Kaplan with enthusiasm.

"No, no," said Mr. Parkhill hastily. "The assignment was *meant* to be a composition. You see, we must begin with simple exercises before we try—er—more philosophical essays."

Mr. Kaplan nodded with resignation. "So naxt time should be no ideas, like abot Shaksbeer? Should be only *fects?*"

"Y-yes. No ideas, only—er—facts."

You could see by Mr. Kaplan's martyred smile that his wings, like those of an eagle, were being clipped.

"And Mr. Kaplan—er—why do you use 'Kaplan' in the body of your composition? Why don't you say *'I* will make the foreman a cutter' instead of *'Kaplan* will make the foreman a cutter?' "

Mr. Kaplan's response was instantaneous. "I'm so glad you eskink me dis! Ha! I'm usink 'Keplen' in de composition for plain and tsimple rizzon: becawss I didn't vant de reader should tink I am *prajudiced* aganst de foreman, so I said it more like abot a strenger: '*Keplen* vill make de foreman a cotter!' "

In the face of this subtle passion for objectivity, Mr. Parkhill was silent. He called for corrections. A forest of hands went up. Miss Mitnick pointed out errors in spelling, the use of capital letters, punctuation; Mr. Norman Bloom corrected several more words, rearranged sentences, and said, "Woikers is exployted with an '*i*,' not 'y' as Kaplan makes"; Miss Caravello changed "fulls" to "fools," and declared herself uncertain as to the validity of the word "Justice" standing by itself in "da smalla da sentence"; Mr. Sam Pinsky said he was sure Mr. Kaplan meant "*opprassed* voikers of de voild, not *deprassed*, aldough dey are deprassed *too*," to which Mr. Kaplan replied, "So ve bote got right, no? Don' *chenge* 'deprassed,' only *add* 'opprassed.' "

Then Mr. Parkhill went ahead with his own corrections, changing tenses, substituting prepositions, adding the definite article. Through the whole barrage Mr. Kaplan kept shaking his head, murmuring "Mine gootness!" each time a correction was made. But he smiled all the while. He seemed to be proud of the very number of errors he had made; of the labor to which the class was being forced in his service; of the fact that his *ideas*, his creation, could survive so concerted an onslaught. And as the composition took more respectable form, Mr. Kaplan's smile grew more expansive.

"Now, class," said Mr. Parkhill, "I want to spend a few minutes explaining something about adjectives. Mr. Kaplan uses the phrase—er—'most bad.' That's wrong. There is a word for 'most bad.' It is what we call the superlative form of 'bad.' " Mr. Parkhill explained the use of the positive, comparative, and superlative forms of the adjective. " 'Tall, taller, tallest.' 'Rich, richer, richest.' Is that clear? Well then, let us try a few others."

The class took up the game with enthusiasm. Miss Mitnick submitted "dark, darker, darkest"; Mr. Scymzak, "fat, fatter, fattest."

"But there are certain exceptions to this general form," Mr. Parkhill went on. The class, which had long ago learned to respect that gamin, The Exception to the Rule, nodded solemnly. "For instance, we don't say 'good, gooder, goodest,' do we?"

"No, sir!" cried Mr. Kaplan impetuously. " 'Good, gooder, good*est*?' Ha! It's to leff!"

"We say that X, for example, is good. Y, however, is—?" Mr. Parkhill arched an eyebrow interrogatively.

"Batter!" said Mr. Kaplan.

"Right! And Z is—?"

"High-cless!"

Mr. Parkhill's eyebrow dropped. "No," he said sadly.

"*Not* high-cless?" asked Mr. Kaplan incredulously. For him there was no word more superlative.

"No, Mr. Kaplan, the word is 'best.' And the word 'bad,' of which you tried to use the superlative form . . . It isn't *bad, badder, baddest.* It's 'bad' . . . and what's the comparative? Anyone?"

"Worse," volunteered Mr. Bloom.

"Correct! And the superlative? Z is the—?"

" 'Worse' also?" asked Mr. Bloom hesitantly. It was evident he had never distinguished the fine difference in sound between the comparative and superlative forms of "bad."

"No, Mr. Bloom. It's not the *same* word, although it—er—sounds a good deal like it. Anyone? Come, come. It isn't hard. X is *bad*, Y is *worse*, and Z is the—?"

An embarrassed silence fell upon the class, which, apparently, had been using "worse" for both the comparative and superlative all along. Miss Mitnick blushed and played with her pencil. Mr. Bloom shrugged, conscious that he had given his all. Mr. Kaplan stared at the board, his mouth open, a desperate concentration in his eye.

"*Bad—worse.* What is the word you use when you mean 'most bad'?"

"Aha!" cried Mr. Kaplan suddenly. When Mr.

Kaplan cried "Aha!" it signified that a great light had fallen on him. "I know! De exect void! So easy! *Ach!* I should know dat ven I vas wridink! *Bad— voise—*"

"Yes, Mr. Kaplan!" Mr. Parkhill was definitely excited.

"Rotten!"

Mr. Parkhill's eyes glazed once more, unmistakably. He shook his head dolorously, as if he had suffered a personal hurt. And as he wrote "w-o-r-s-t" on the blackboard there ran through his head, like a sad refrain, this latest manifestation of Mr. Kaplan's peculiar genius: "bad—worse—rotten; bad— worse . . ."

MR. K*A*P*L*A*N'S
HOBO

PERHAPS Mr. Parkhill should have known better. Perhaps he should have known Mr. Kaplan better. And yet, in Mr. Parkhill's conscientious concern for *every* student in the beginners' grade there could be no discrimination. Despite Mr. Kaplan's distressing class record, despite his amazing renditions of the English language, Mr. Parkhill insisted on treating him as any other student. Just because Mr. Kaplan referred to rubber heels as "robber hills," or called a pencil-sharpener a "pantsil-chopner," was no reason he should not participate in the regular exercises of the class on an equal footing. (Mr. Parkhill had weakened a bit in this resolution when Mr. Kaplan had given the opposite of "new" as "second hand.")

And now Mr. Kaplan stood at the front of the room before the class, ready to speak for five minutes during the Recitation and Speech period.

"Speak slowly, Mr. Kaplan," said Mr. Parkhill. "Watch your pronunciation. Remember it isn't how

—er—*fast* you talk, or how *much* you say. Try to be accurate. Speak distinctly."

Mr. Kaplan nodded with a great and confident smile.

"And do watch your 'e's and 'a's. You always confuse them in your speech."

Mr. Kaplan nodded again, beaming. "I'll be so careful, Mr. Pockhill, you'll be soprize," he said gallantly.

"And the class will feel free to interrupt with corrections at any time." Mr. Parkhill finished his instructions with an encouraging nod to the class. Allowing the students to interrupt with corrections had proved very successful. It kept them alert, and it made the student reciting particularly careful, since there was a certain stigma attached to being corrected by a fellow-student—much greater than if Mr. Parkhill did the correcting. It was natural for *him* to catch errors.

"Very well, Mr. Kaplan." Mr. Parkhill sighed, aware that he could do no more. Now it was in the hands of God. He took Mr. Kaplan's seat. (He always took the seat of the student reciting during Recitation and Speech period. It seemed to establish a comradely rapport in the class; besides, it was easier to hear and watch the student speaking.)

Mr. Kaplan took a deep breath. For a suspended moment he surveyed the class. There was pride in his glance. Mr. Kaplan loved to recite. He loved to write on the blackboard. In fact, he loved any activity in which he was the single center of attention. He laughed a strange, soft, rather meaningless laugh. Then he began:

"Ladies an' gantleman—I s'pose dat's how I should beginnink—an' also Mr. Pockheel an' faller-students—"

He cleared his throat, almost with a flourish.

"Eh—I'm spikking tonight becawss it's Rasitation an' Spitch time an'—"

"Sp*ee*ch, Mr. Kaplan," Mr. Parkhill interpolated gently. "Watch your 'e's."

"Becawss it's Rasitation an' Sp*eeee*ch time, so I'll talkink abot mine vaca—no—*my* vacation." Mr. Kaplan corrected himself, smiling, as he saw Mr. Parkhill frown. "So is de name fromm my leetle spi—sp*eeee*ch: My Vacation!"

Mr. Kaplan stopped sententiously. He had a keen sense of structure.

"Foist, I must tell abot my hobo."

The class, with the fervent intensity with which it listened to students reciting, looked puzzled. So did Mr. Parkhill.

"My hobo is—"

"Your—er—*what?*" asked Mr. Parkhill anxiously.

"My hobo."

"No soch woid!" cried Mr. Norman Bloom. Whenever Mr. Bloom suspected an error in vocabulary, he jumped to the conclusion that there was "no soch woid." It was the safest tactic.

"Oh, no?" asked Mr. Kaplan, smiling. "Maybe you *positif?*"

"Well, there is such a word," said Mr. Parkhill, quickly. "But—er—are you sure you *mean* 'hobo'?"

"Aha!" Mr. Kaplan cried triumphantly, looking at Mr. Bloom. "So *is* soch a void! Vell, I tink I minn 'hobo.' My hobo is hiking—hiking in de voods, or on de heels, or op de montains—all kinds hiking. Venever is a fine day, mit sonshinink, I go hiking in—"

"He means 'hobby,'" hissed Miss Rose Mitnick to Mrs. Rodriguez. Miss Mitnick was a shy girl. Ordinarily she did not volunteer corrections, although she was the best student in the class. But between Miss Mitnick and Mr. Kaplan there was

something of a feud. Mr. Kaplan heard Miss Mitnick's hiss. So did everyone else.

"So I'm corracted by Mitnick," said Mr. Kaplan
generously. "Is not my '*hobo*.' My *hobby*— Hau
Kay! But Bloom shouldn't say dere's no void '*hobo*.'
It's only *annoder* void, dat's all."

Mr. Bloom was impotent against this sophistry.
Mr. Kaplan smiled graciously at both Miss Mitnick
and Mr. Bloom, with the faintest suggestion of irony.
Suddenly he straightened up. His smile grew wider,
almost beatific. An exalted look came into his eyes.
With a sudden motion he stretched both hands out-
ward and cried, "De sky! De son! De stoss! De
clods. De frash air in de longs. All—all is pot fromm
Netcher!"

A reverent hush fell over the class as Mr. Kaplan
depicted the glories of Nature.

"An' do ve human fools taking edwantage? No!"

Miss Mitnick blushed as if she were personally
responsible for man's indifference to the out-of-doors.

"But in hiking is all enjoymint fromm soch
Netcher. Dat's vy I'm makink a hobby fromm hiking.
Ladies an' gantleman, have you one an' all, or even
saparate, falt *in de soul* de trees, de boids, de gress,
de bloomers—all de scinnery?"

A swift titter from the ladies made Mr. Kaplan pause, his hands arrested in mid-air.

"Yas, de trees, de boids, de gress, de bloomers—"

"Er—pardon me," said Mr. Parkhill, clearly embarrassed. "But what word *are* you using, Mr. Kaplan?"

"All kinds," Mr. Kaplan said with sublime simplicity.

"But—er—you used one word—"

" 'Bloomers' ain't natural hobjects!" blurted Mrs. Moskowitz firmly. Mrs. Moskowitz was a straightforward, earthy soul. And, as a married woman, she could speak out where Mr. Parkhill or the class might hesitate. "You mean 'flowers,' Mr. Kaplan, so don't mix op two languages!"

Mr. Parkhill, who had thought that Mr. Kaplan's use of "bloomers" came from a misconstruction of the verb "to bloom," naïvely transformed into a noun, suddenly recalled that *Blumen* meant "flowers" in Mr. Kaplan's native tongue.

"Hau Kay!" said Mr. Kaplan, promptly. "So podden me an' denk you! Is de void batter 'flower.' So I love to smallink de flowers, like Moskovitz said. I love to breedink de frash air. Mostly, I love to hear de boids sinking."

"You *must* watch your 'k's and 'g's," said Mr. Parkhill earnestly. " 'Singing,' not 'sin*k*ing.' "

Mr. Kaplan lifted his eyebrows with a responsive "Ah!"

"An' ven de boids is sin*g*ing, den is Netcher commink ot in all kinds gorgeous."

Mr. Parkhill looked at the floor; there was no point in being picayune.

"Vell, lest veek I took my vife ot to de contry. I told my vife, 'Sarah, you should have an absolutel vacation. Slip—eat—valk aron' in Netcher. Stay in de bad how late you vant in de mornink!' But my vife! *Ach!* Did she slapt late? No! Not my Sarah. Avery mornink she got op six o'clock, no matter vat time it vas!"

For a moment there was a stunned silence. Then Miss Mitnick interrupted with shy but firm determination. She did not look at Mr. Kaplan. She addressed her words to Mr. Parkhill—rather, to Mr. Parkhill's tie. "How can Mr. Kaplan say she got up every morning at six o'clock 'no matter what time it was'? A mistake."

The class nodded, the full meaning of Mr. Kaplan's paradox sinking in.

"Yes," said Mr. Parkhill. "I'm sure you didn't mean that, Mr. Kaplan."

Mr. Kaplan's great smile did not leave his face for a moment. He looked at Miss Mitnick through half-closed eyes and, with infinite superiority, said, "I have a foist-cless idea vat I'm minnink, Mitnick. My vife gats op so oily in de mornink dat *you* couldn't tell vat time it vas, *I* couldn't tell vat time it vas, even Mr. Pockheel couldn't tell. Avery day in de contry she vas gattink op six o'clock, *no matter vat time it vas.*"

Miss Mitnick's blush was heart-rending.

"Don' be like that, Kaplan!" exclaimed Mr. Bloom, jumping into the gap chivalrously. "If it's six o'clock, so you *do* know what time it was, no? So how you can say—"

"Aha!" Mr. Kaplan cried defiantly. "Dat's exactel de mistake you makink just like Mitnick. If I'm *slippink* an' it's six o'clock, so do *I* know vat time it is? Vould *you* know it vas six o'clock if *you* vas slippink?"

It was a dazzling dialectical stroke. It silenced Mr. Kaplan's critics with instant and deadly accuracy. Mr. Bloom pursed his lips, a miserable man. Miss Mitnick frowned and flushed, such metaphysical rea-

soning quite beyond her. Mrs. Moskowitz's eyes held
awe for Mr. Kaplan's devastating logic. It remained
for Mr. Parkhill to break through the impasse.

"But—er—Mr. Kaplan, if one *states* the time as
six o'clock, then it's incorrect to add 'no matter
what time it was.' That's a contradiction."

The class sat breathless. Mr. Kaplan's smile
seemed ossified for one long moment as he looked
at Mr. Parkhill. Then it flowed into life and peace
again. "Oh, vell. If it's a *conterdiction*"—he looked
haughtily at Miss Mitnick and Mr. Bloom—"dat's
difference!"

Mr. Bloom nodded in acquiescence, as if he under-
stood this masterful denouement; he tried to achieve
a profound expression. A bewildered look crept into
Miss Mitnick's eyes.

Mr. Kaplan beamed. He put his hands out dramatically and exclaimed, "How many you fine city
pipple ever saw de son commink op? How many you
children fromm Netcher smalled de gress in de
mornink all vet mit dues? How many—"

Just then the bell rang in the corridors of the
American Night Preparatory School for Adults. Mr.
Kaplan stopped, his hand in mid-air—like a gull
coasting. The class seemed suspended, like the hand.

"I'm afraid the period's up," said Mr. Parkhill.

Mr. Kaplan sighed philosophically, took his hand-kerchief from his pocket, and wiped the perspiration from his brow. "Vell, denks Gott dat's de and fromm de spi-sp*ee*ch of—" he drew himself erect—"Hymen Keplen."

As Mr. Kaplan uttered his own name, as if he were referring to some celebrity known to them all, Mr. Parkhill, by some visual conditioned reflex, *saw* the name. He saw it just as Mr. Kaplan always wrote it. It seemed impossible, fantastic, yet Mr. Kaplan had *pronounced* his name in red and blue and green: H * Y * M * A * N   K * A * P * L * A * N.

Mr. Parkhill sat quite still, thinking, as the class filed out.

MR. K*A*P*L*A*N
AND VOCABULARY

"VOCABULARY!" said Mr. Parkhill. "Above all, we must work on vocabulary."

He was probably right. For the students in the beginners' grade, vocabulary was a dire and pressing need. Spelling, after all, was not of such immediate importance to people who did little writing during their daily lives. Grammar? They needed the substance—words, phrases, idioms—to which grammar might be applied. Pronunciation? Mr. Parkhill had come to the reluctant conclusion that for some of them accurate pronunciation was a near impossibility. Take Mr. Kaplan, for example. Mr. Kaplan was a willing, an earnest, aye! an enthusiastic pupil. And yet, despite Mr. Parkhill's tireless tutelage, Mr. Kaplan referred to the most celebrated of movie lovers as "Clock Gebble," who, it appeared, showed a fine set of teeth "venever he greens." Mr. Kaplan, when asked to use "heaven" in a sentence, had replied promptly, "In sommer, ve all heaven a fine time."

Yes, vocabulary—that, Mr. Parkhill thought, was the greatest need.

". . . And so tonight I shall write a list of new, useful words on the blackboard. To each student I shall assign three words. Write a sentence in your notebooks using each word. Make sure you have no mistakes. You may use your dictionaries, if you wish. Then go to the board and copy your three sentences for class analysis."

The class was impressed and pleased. Miss Mitnick's ordinarily shy expression changed to one of eager expectancy. Mrs. Moskowitz, simple soul that she was, prepared her notebook with stolid solemnity. And Mr. Kaplan, in the middle of the front row, took out his box of crayons, smiled more broadly than ever (a chance to use his crayons always intensified Mr. Kaplan's natural euphoria), turned to a fresh page in his notebook, and printed, slowly and with great love:

VOCAPULERY
(Prectice in Book. Then Going to Blackb. and putting on.)
by
H * Y * M * A * N   K * A * P * L * A * N

For the title he chose purple crayon; for the methodological observation in parentheses, orange; for the "by," yellow. His name he printed, fondly, as always: in red and blue and flamboyant green. As he handled the crayons Mr. Kaplan smiled with the sweet serenity of one in direct communication with his Muse.

Mr. Parkhill assigned three words to each student and the beginners' grade went into action. Lips pursed, brows wrinkled, distant looks appeared in thoughtful eyes; heads were scratched, chins stroked, dictionaries fluttered. Mr. Kaplan tackled his three words with gusto: *pitcher, fascinate, university.* Mr. Parkhill noticed that Mr. Kaplan's cerebration was accompanied by strange sounds: he pronounced each word, and tried fitting it into a sentence, in a whisper which could be heard halfway across the room. He muttered the entire process of his reasoning. Mr. Kaplan, it seemed, thought only in dialogue with his other self. There was something uncanny about it.

"Pitcher . . . pitcher," Mr. Kaplan whispered. "Is maybe a pitcher for milk? Is maybe a pitcher on de vall—*art!* Aha! Two minninks! 'Plizz take milk fromm de pitcher.' Fine! 'De pitcher hengs cockeye.' Also fine! Pitcher . . . pitcher."

This private colloquy was not indulged in without a subtle design, for Mr. Kaplan watched Mr. Parkhill's facial expressions carefully out of the corner of his eye as he whispered to himself. Mr. Kaplan hoped to discover which interpretation of "pitcher" was acceptable. But Mr. Parkhill had long ago learned to beware of Mr. Kaplan's strategies; he preserved a stern facial immobility as Mr. Kaplan's stage whispers floated through the classroom.

When Mr. Kaplan had finished his three sentences he reread them proudly, nodded happily to Mr. Parkhill (who, though pretending to be watching Miss Schneiderman at the blackboard, was watching Mr. Kaplan out of the corner of *his* eye), and went to the board. He whispered the sentences aloud as he copied them. Ecstasy illuminated his face.

"Well," said Mr. Parkhill after all the students had transcribed their work, "let's start at this end. Mr. Bloom, I think?"

Mr. Bloom read his sentences quickly:

> She *declined* the money.
> In her red hat she falt *conspicuous.*
> Last Saturday, I saw a *remarkable* show.

"Excellent!" said Mr. Parkhill. "Are there any questions?" There were no questions. Mr. Parkhill corrected "falt" and the exercise continued. On the whole, all went surprisingly well. Except for those of Mrs. Moskowitz, who worked havoc with "niggardly" ("It was a *niggardly* night"), the sentences were quite good. Mr. Parkhill was delighted. The experiment in vocabulary-building was proving a decided success. At last Mr. Kaplan's three sentences came up.

"Mr. Kaplan is next, I believe." There was a note of caution in Mr. Parkhill's voice.

Mr. Kaplan went to the board. "Mine foist void, ladies an' gantleman," he announced, smiling (Mr. Kaplan always did things with a certain bravado), "is 'pitcher.' So de santence is: 'Oh, how beauriful is dis *pitcher.*'"

Mr. Parkhill saw that Mr. Kaplan had neatly straddled two words by a deliberately noncommittal usage. "Er—Mr. Kaplan. The word is 'p-i-t-c-h-e-r,' not 'p-i-c-t-u-r-e.'"

Too late did Mr. Parkhill realize that he had given Mr. Kaplan the clue he had been seeking.

"Mr. Pockheel," Mr. Kaplan replied with consummate simplicity, "dis void *is* 'p-i-t-c-h-e-r.'"

"But when you say, 'Oh, how *beautiful* this pitcher is,'" said Mr. Parkhill, determined to force Mr. Kaplan to the wall, "you suggest—"

"Ah!" Mr. Kaplan murmured, with a tolerant

smile. "In som houses is even de *pitchers* beauriful."

"Read your next sentence, Mr. Kaplan."

Mr. Kaplan went on, smiling. "De sacond void, ladies an' gantleman, is 'fascinate'—an' believe me is a planty hod void! So is mine santence: 'In India is all kinds snake-fescinators.' "

"You are thinking of snake-*charmers*." (Mr. Kaplan seemed to have taken the dictionary's description of "fascinate" too literally.) "Try 'fascinate' in another sentence, please."

Mr. Kaplan gazed ceilingward with a masterful insouciance, one eye half-closed. Then he ventured: "You *fescinate* me."

Mr. Parkhill hurried Mr. Kaplan on to his last word.

"Toid void, faller-students, is 'univoisity.' De santence usink dis void: 'Elaven yiss is married mine vife an' minesalf, so is time commink for our tvalft *univoisity*.' "

It was the opportunity for which Miss Mitnick had been waiting. "Mr. Kaplan mixes up two words," she said. "He means 'anniversary.' 'University' is a high college—the *highest* college."

Mr. Kaplan listened to this unwelcome correction with a fine sufferance. Then he arched his eyebrows

and said, "You got right, Mitnick. Hau Kay! So I'll
givink anodder santence: 'Som pipple didn't have
aducation in a *univoisity*' "—he glanced meaning-
fully at Miss Mitnick—" 'but just de same, dey havink efter elaven yiss de tvalft *annivoisery.*' "

With this retort courteous Mr. Kaplan took his
seat. Through the next few recitations he was
strangely silent. He did not bother to offer a correction of Miss Kowalski's spectacular misuse of "guess."
("Turn out the guess.") He did not as much as volunteer an opinion on Miss Hirschfield's "The cat
omits a cry." For all his proud smile it was clear that
Mr. Kaplan had suffered a deep hurt: like a smolder-
ing cinder in his soul lay the thought of his humilia-
tion at the mundane hands of one Rose Mitnick. He
smiled as bravely as ever, but his silence was ominous. He seemed to be waiting, waiting. . . .

"Miss Mitnick, please," said Mr. Parkhill. A
flame leaped into Mr. Kaplan's eyes.

Miss Mitnick's first sentence was *"Enamel* is used
for painting chairs." Before she could read it Mr.
Kaplan's voice rang out in triumph.

"Mistake by Mitnick! Ha! Mit *enimals* she is
painting chairs? Ha!"

"The word is *'enamel,'* " said Mr. Parkhill coldly.
"Not 'animal.' "

Rebuffed, Mr. Kaplan let Miss Mitnick's reading
of that sentence, and her next, go unchallenged. But
the flame burned in his eyes again when she read her
final effort: "The prisoner stood in the *dock.*"

"Well," suggested Mr. Parkhill, before Mr. Kaplan, squirming with excitement in his chair, could
offer a rash correction, "that's one way to use the
word. The English use it that way. But there is a—
er—more common usage. Can you use 'dock' in a
more familiar meaning, Miss Mitnick?"

Miss Mitnick was silent.

"Anyone?"

"I like roast *duck!*" cried Mr. Kaplan promptly.

"*Dock!*" Mr. Parkhill said severely. "Not *duck!*"
Once again Mr. Kaplan bowed to a cruel fate.

" 'Dock' isn't hard," said Mr. Parkhill encouragingly. "I'll give you a hint, class. Each of you, in
coming to America, has had *direct experience with a
dock.*" He smiled almost gaily, and waited.

The class went into that coma which signified
thought, searching its collective memory of "coming
to America." Mrs. Moskowitz closed her eyes as the
recollection of her sea-sickness surged over her like a

wave, and searched her memory no more. Mr.
Kaplan, desperate to make the kill, whispered his
associations tensely: " 'Dock' . . . Commink to
America . . . boat . . . feesh . . . big vaves . . .
cremps."

It was clear they were getting nowhere. (Mr.
Norman Bloom, indeed, had forgotten all about
"dock" in his sweet recollection of the pinochle game
on the boat when he had won four and a half dol-
lars.)

"Well, I'll make it even easier," said Mr. Parkhill lightly. "Where did your boats *land?*"

"New York!" cried Mr. Kaplan eagerly.

Mr. Parkhill cleared his throat. "Yes—of course.
But I mean—"

A cry of joy came from the lips of Hyman Kaplan. "I got him! Ufcawss! *'Dock!'* Plain an' tsimple!
Ha!" He shot a look of triumph toward Miss Mitnick. "I'm soprize so high-cless a student like Mitnick, she knows all abot fency voids like 'univoisities'
and 'annivoiseries,' she shouldn't know a leetle void
like 'dock'!"

Something in Mr. Parkhill warned him. Not for a
moment could he believe that Mr. Kaplan's confidence and enthusiasm were authentic indications of a

correct answer. Mr. Parkhill would have preferred that some other student try a sentence with "dock." But no one volunteered.

"Very well, Mr. Kaplan," he said, staring at his fingers, as if to break the impact of Mr. Kaplan's contribution.

Mr. Kaplan rose, inspiration in his eyes. His smile was so wide that his face seemed to be one ecstatic cavern. He cast majestic glances to both sides, as if reading the tribute in the faces of his fellow-students. Then he said, in one triumphant breath, "Hollo, Doc!"

Peace fell upon the room. Through the windows, from far away, there came the muted rumble of the Third Avenue elevated. The features of Abraham Lincoln on the wall took on, somehow, a softer understanding. But Mr. Parkhill was aware only of a strange and unaccountable ringing in his ears ("Hello, Doc!" . . . "Hello, Doc!") and, while shaking his head sadly to show Mr. Kaplan that he was wrong, he thought to himself with feverish persistence, "Vocabulary. Above all, vocabulary."

MR. K*A*P*L*A*N
THE MAGNIFICENT

MR. PARKHILL had decided that perhaps it might be wise for the class to attempt more *practical* exercises. On a happy thought, he had taken up the subject of letter-writing. He had lectured the students on the general structure of the personal letter: shown them where to put the address, city, date; explained the salutation; talked about the body of the letter; described the final greeting. And now the fruits of Mr. Parkhill's labors were being demonstrated. Five students had written the assignment, "A Letter to a Friend," on the blackboard.

On the whole Mr. Parkhill was satisfied. Miss Mitnick had a straightforward and accurate letter—as might be expected—inviting her friend Sylvia to a surprise party. Mr. Norman Bloom had written to someone named Fishbein, describing an exciting day at Coney Island. Miss Rochelle Goldberg had told "Molly" about a "bos ride on a bos on 5 av." Mrs. Moskowitz, simple soul, had indulged her fantasies by pretending she was on vacation in "Miame, Floridal," and had written her husband Oscar to be sure "the pussy should get each morning milk." (Apparently Mrs. Moskowitz was deeply attached to "the pussy," for she merely repeated the admonition in several ways all through her epistle, leaving no room for comment on the beauties of "Miame, Floridal.") And Mr. Hyman Kaplan—Mr. Parkhill frowned as he examined the last letter written on the blackboard.

"It's to mine brodder in Varsaw," said Mr. Kaplan, smiling in happy anticipation.

Mr. Parkhill nodded, rather absently; his eyes were fixed on the board.

"Maybe it vould be easier I should readink de ladder alod," suggested Mr. Kaplan delicately.

" '*Letter*,' Mr. Kaplan," said Mr. Parkhill, ever the pedagogue. "Not '*lad*der.' "

"Maybe I should readink de *lat*ter?" repeated Mr. Kaplan.

"Er—no—no," said Mr. Parkhill hastily. "We—er—we haven't much time left this evening. It *is* getting late." He tried to put it as gently as possible, knowing what this harsh deprivation might mean to Mr. Kaplan's soul.

Mr. Kaplan sighed philosophically, bowing to the tyranny of time.

"The class will study the letter for a few minutes, please," said Mr. Parkhill. "Then I shall call for corrections."

The class fell into that half-stupor which indicated concentration. Miss Mitnick studied the blackboard with a determined glint in her eye. Mr. Pinsky stared at Mr. Kaplan's letter with a critical air, saying "Tchk! Tchk!" several times, quite professionally. Mrs. Moskowitz gazed ceilingward with an exhausted expression. Apparently the vicarious excitements of the class session had been too much for poor Mrs. Moskowitz: an invitation to a surprise party, a thrilling day at Coney Island, a Fifth Avenue bus ride, and her own trip to Florida. That was quite a night for Mrs. Moskowitz.

And Mr. Kaplan sat with his joyous smile unmarred, a study in obvious pride and simulated modesty, like a god to whom mortals were paying homage. First he watched the faces of the students as they wrestled with his handiwork, and found them pleasing. Then he concentrated his gaze on Mr. Parkhill. He saw anxious little lines creep around Mr. Parkhill's eyes as he read that letter; then a frown—a strange frown, bewildered and incredulous; then a nervous clearing of the throat. Any other student might have been plunged into melancholy by these dark omens, but they only added a transcendental quality to Mr. Kaplan's smile.

This was the letter Mr. Kaplan had written:

459 E 3 Str
N.Y.
New York
Octo. 10

HELLO MAX!!!

I should telling about mine progriss. In school I am fine. Making som mistakes, netcheral. Also however doing the hardest xrcises, like the best students the same. Som students is Mitnick, Blum, Moskowitz—no relation Moskowitz in Warsaw. Max! You should absolutel coming to N.Y. and belonging in mine school!

It was at this point, visualizing too vividly *another* Mr. Kaplan in the class, that anxious little lines had crept around Mr. Parkhill's eyes.

Do you feeling fine? I suppose. Is all ok? You should begin right now learning about ok. Here you got to say ok. all the time. ok the wether, ok the potatos, ok the prazident Roosevelt.

At this point the frown—a strange frown, bewildered and incredulous—had marched onto Mr. Parkhill's face.

How is darling Fanny? Long should she leave. So long.
With all kinds entusiasm

Your animated brother

H * Y * M * I * E

Mr. Kaplan simply could not resist the aesthetic impulse to embellish his signature with those stars; they had almost become an integral part of the name itself.

Mr. Parkhill cleared his throat. He felt vaguely distressed.

"Has everyone finished reading?" he asked. Heads nodded in half-hearted assent. "Well, let us begin. Corrections, please."

Mrs. Tomasic's hand went up. "Should be 'N.Y.' after 'New York' and 'New York' should be on top of."

"Correct," said Mr. Parkhill, explaining the difference and making the change on the board.

"In all places is 'mine' wrong," said Mr. Feigenbaum. "It should be 'my.'"

Mr. Parkhill nodded, happy that someone had

caught that most common of Mr. Kaplan's errors.

The onslaught went on: the spelling of words, the abbreviation of "October" and "street," the tenses of the verbs.

"Mr. Kaplan got so many mistakes," began Mr. Bloom with hauteur. Mr. Bloom was still annoyed because Mr. Kaplan had rashly offered to correct the spelling of Coney Island, in Mr. Bloom's letter, to " 'Corney Island,' like is pernonced." "He spelled wrong 'progress,' 'some,' 'natural.' He means 'Long should she *live*'—not 'Long should she *leave.*' That means going away. He even spelled wrong my name!" It was clear from Mr. Bloom's indignant tone that this was by far the most serious of Mr. Kaplan's many errors. "Is double 'o,' not 'u.' I ain't like *som* Blooms!"

With this jealous defence of the honor of the House of Bloom, Mr. Bloom looked at Mr. Kaplan coolly. If he had thought to see Mr. Kaplan chagrined by the barrage of corrections he did not know the real mettle of the man. Mr. Kaplan was beaming with delight.

"Honist to Gott, Bloom," said Mr. Kaplan with admiration, "you soitinly improvink in your English to seeink all dese mistakes!"

There was a fine charity in this accolade. It had, however, the subtle purpose of shifting attention from Mr. Kaplan's errors to Mr. Bloom's progress.

Mr. Bloom did not know whether to be pleased or suspicious, whether this was a glowing tribute or the most insidious irony.

"Thenks, Kaplan," he said finally, acknowledging the compliment with a nod, and considered the injuries of "Corney Island" and "Blum" expiated.

"I see more mistakes," said Miss Mitnick, intruding an unwelcome note into the happy Kaplan-Bloom rapport. Mr. Kaplan's eyes gleamed when he heard Miss Mitnick's voice. Here was a foe of a caliber quite different from that of Norman Bloom. " 'Absolutel' should be 'absolutely.' 'Potatoes' has an 'e.' 'Prazident' is wrong; it should be 'e' and 's' and a capital." Miss Mitnick went on and on making corrections. Mr. Parkhill transcribed them to the board as swiftly as he could, until his wrists began to ache. " 'ok' is wrong, should be 'O.K.'—with *capitals* and *periods*—because it's abbreviation."

All through the Mitnick attack Mr. Kaplan sat quiet, alert but smiling. There was a supreme confidence in that smile, as if he were waiting for some secret opportunity to send the whole structure that

Miss Mitnick was rearing so carefully crashing down upon her head. Miss Mitnick rushed on to the abyss.

"Last," she said, slowing up to emphasize the blow, "*three* exclamation points after 'Max' is wrong. Too many."

"Aha!" cried Mr. Kaplan. It was The Opportunity. "Podden me, Mitnick. De odder corractinks you makink is fine, foist-class—even Hau Kay, an' I minn Hau Kay mit *capitals* an' *periods*," he added sententiously. "But batter takink back abot de tree haxclimation points!"

Miss Mitnick blushed, looking to Mr. Parkhill for succor.

"Mr. Kaplan," said Mr. Parkhill with caution, sensing some hidden logic in Mr. Kaplan's tone. "A colon is the proper punctuation for the salutation, or a comma. If you *must* use an—er—exclamation point"—he was guarding himself on all fronts—"then, as Miss Mitnick says, *three* are too many."

"For de vay *I'm* fillink abot mine *brodder?*" asked Mr. Kaplan promptly. In that question, sublime in its simplicity, Mr. Kaplan inferentially accused his detractor of (1) familial ingratitude, (2) trying to come between the strong love of two brothers.

"But, Kaplan," broke in Mr. Bloom, jumping into

the fray on the side of Miss Mitnick, "*three* ex-
clama—"

"Also he's mine *faworite* brodder!" said Mr. Kaplan. "For mine *faworite* brodder you eskink *vun—*
leetle—haxclimation point?" It was an invincible position. "Ha! Dat I give to *strengers!*"

Mr. Bloom retired from the field, annihilated.
One could hardly expect a man of Mr. Kaplan's
exquisite sensitivity to give equal deference and love
to *strangers* and his favorite brother. Mr. Parkhill
paused to mobilize his forces.

"How's about 'entusiasm'?" said Miss Mitnick,
determined to recover face. "Is spelled wrong—
should be 'th.' And 'With all kinds enthusiasm' is
bad for ending a letter."

"Aha!" Mr. Kaplan gave his battle call again.
"Maybe *is* de spallink wronk. But not de vay I'm
usink 'antusiasm,' becawss—"—he injected a tren-
chant quality into his voice to let the class get the
deepest meaning of his next remark—"becawss *I*
write to *mine* brodder in Varsaw *mit real antusiasm!*"

The implication was clear: Miss Mitnick was one
of those who, corrupted by the gaudy whirl of the
New World, let her brothers starve, indifferently,
overseas.

Miss Mitnick bit her lip. Mr. Parkhill, trying to look judicious, avoided her eyes.

"Well," began Miss Mitnick yet a third time, desperately, " 'animated' is wrong. 'Your *animated* brother, Hymie?' *That's* wrong."

She looked at Mr. Parkhill with a plea that was poignant. She dared not look at Mr. Kaplan, whose smile had advanced to a new dimension.

"Yes," said Mr. Parkhill. " 'Animated' is quite out of place in the final greeting."

Mr. Kaplan sighed. "I looked op de void 'enimated' *spacial*. It's minnink 'full of life,' no? Vell, I falt *planty* full of life ven I vas wridink de ladder."

Miss Mitnick dropped her eyes, the rout complete.

"Mr. Kaplan!" Mr. Parkhill was left to fight the good fight alone. "You may say 'She had an animated expression' or 'The music has an animated refrain.' But one doesn't say 'animated' about one's *self*."

The appeal to propriety proved successful. Mr. Kaplan confessed that perhaps he had overreached himself with "Your animated brother."

"Suppose we try another word," suggested Mr. Parkhill. "How about 'fond'? 'Your *fond* brother—er—Hyman?' " (He couldn't quite essay "Hymie.")

Mr. Kaplan half-closed his eyes, gazed into space, and meditated on this moot point. " 'Fond,' 'fond,' " he whispered to himself. He was like a man who had retreated into a secret world, searching for his Muse. " 'Your fond brodder, Hymie.' " He shook his head. "Podden me," he said apologetically. "It don' have de *fillink*."

"What about 'dear'?" offered Mr. Parkhill quickly. " 'Your *dear* brother,' and so on?"

Once more Mr. Kaplan went through the process of testing, judgment, and consultation with his evasive Muse. " 'Dear,' 'dear,' 'Your dear brodder, Hymie.' Also no." He sighed. " 'Dear,' it's too *common*."

"What about—"

"Aha!" cried Mr. Kaplan suddenly, as the Muse kissed him. His smile was as the sun. "I got him! Fine! Poifick! Soch a void!"

The class, to whom Mr. Kaplan had communicated some of his own excitement, waited breathlessly. Mr. Parkhill himself, it might be said, was possessed of a queer eagerness.

"Yes, Mr. Kaplan. What word would you suggest?"

" 'Megnificent!' " cried Mr. Kaplan.

Admiration and silence fell upon the class like a benediction. "Your magnificent brother, Hymie." It was a *coup de maître,* no less. Mr. K*A*P-L*A*N the Magnificent.

As if in a trance, the beginners' grade waited for Mr. Parkhill's verdict.

And when Mr. Parkhill spoke, it was slowly, sadly, aware that he was breaking a magic spell. "N-no, Mr. Kaplan. I'm afraid not. 'Magnificent' isn't really—er—appropriate."

The bell rang in the corridors, as if it had withheld its signal until the last possible moment. The class moved into life and toward the door. Mr. Norman Bloom went out with Mr. Kaplan. Mr. Parkhill could hear the last words of their conversation.

"Kaplan," said Mr. Bloom enviously, "*how* you fond soch a beautiful woid?"

" 'Megnificent,' 'megnificent,' " Mr. Kaplan murmured to himself wistfully. "Ach! Dat *vas* a beauriful void, ha, Bloom?"

"Believe me!" said Mr. Bloom. "*How* you fond soch a woid?"

"By *dip* tinking," said Mr. Kaplan.

He strode out like a hero.

MR. K*A*P*L*A*N
ALMOST COMES
THROUGH

IT was painfully clear to Mr. Parkhill that Mr. Kaplan's English was long to remain a source of surprise in the beginners' grade. Promotion to Composition, Grammar, and Civics with Miss Higby was, Mr. Parkhill concluded, quite out of the question. It was folly even to think of it.

Every assignment that bore that strange and unmistakable signature, H * Y * M * A * N K * A * P-L * A * N, contained some new and remarkable version of the English language which Mr. Kaplan had determined to master. For Mr. Kaplan was no ordinary student. Mr. Kaplan was no ordinary mortal, for that matter. In his peculiar linguistic universe there was the germ of a new lexicography. To Mr. Kaplan, an instrument for the repair of plumbing was "a monkey ranch"; verbal indiscretions were caused by "a sleeping of the tong"; and, in the sphere of romance, the most attractive women were "female ladies with blondie hairs and blue or maybe gray ice

—like Molly Dietritch." Mr. Parkhill sometimes wondered whether Mr. Kaplan might not be some sort of genius. Isaac Newton, after all, had been considered dull-witted by his teachers.

One night a composition of Miss Mitnick's was up for class analysis. Miss Mitnick had written the assignment on the blackboard. Blushing, with pointer in hand, she read it aloud in a small voice:

My Work—A Waitress

My job is, a waitress in a cafeteria restaurant. I am working nine hours a day. From 7½ in morning to 4½ by night. We are serving there meals, breakfast, lunch (or luncheons, they are smaller), and supper—or dinner as Americans say. My work is, standing behind counter and giving Coffee, Tea, Milk, as customers ask for one. It is not so hard. But I get tired with standing all day and have often headackes. The pay is not so good. But I am happy for having *any* job. We should be happy for having any job. Because all over the world is a depression.

Miss Mitnick stopped. Public performances of any type were an ordeal to Miss Mitnick.

"That's very good," smiled Mr. Parkhill. It *was* very good. Miss Mitnick was easily the best student

in the class. "There are some mistakes, naturally—
in punctuation, in the use of certain prepositions—
but on the whole that is—er—excellent for the beginners' grade."

Miss Mitnick blushed and looked at her pointer.
Mr. Kaplan, in his permanent seat in the front row,
center, nodded tolerant agreement to Mr. Parkhill's
praises: he smiled that broad, happy smile that
bathed his face in blandness.

Mr. Parkhill adjusted his glasses. "Now then, corrections. Please examine the composition carefully,
class. Make a note of any mistakes you see, in your
notebooks. In five minutes I shall call for volun-
teers."

Mr. Parkhill thought this pedagogical technique
very effective; it forced the students to concentrate;
it challenged them. In his chats with Miss Higby,
Mr. Parkhill sometimes told her, with a modest
smile, of "the method of direct participation."

The class became a sea of stares and furrowed
brows as the students applied themselves to Miss
Mitnick's composition. Mrs. Tomasic lowered her
head and examined the floor. Mr. Norman Bloom
jotted several words down swiftly. And Mr. Kaplan,

serene and smiling, took one careless look at the blackboard and began writing in his notebook.

Mr. Parkhill sauntered down the aisle, glancing at the students' desks. "I'll give the class a hint," he said lightly. "There's *one word* spelled wrong."

All looked up, except Mr. Kaplan. He was still preoccupied with the original error he seemed to have caught. His brow was knit, his pencil clutched in hand. He paid no attention to Mr. Parkhill's suggestion. Mr. Kaplan wrote on.

"Er—don't spend too much time on any *one* mistake," announced Mr. Parkhill uneasily. "Just make a note of the error, then examine Miss Mitnick's composition further."

He waited a little while; Mr. Bloom seemed to have caught several more errors. Miss Schneiderman scribbled and smiled knowingly at her friend across the aisle, Carmen Caravello. Still Mr. Kaplan wrote on.

"All right," said Mr. Parkhill. "I think we've had enough time now. Who will be the first volunteer? Corrections?"

Mrs. Moskowitz raised her hand. "Shouldn't be by Miss Mitnick a 'd' on de end 'restaurant'?"

"I'm afraid not," Mr. Parkhill said gently. " 'Restaur*ant*' is correct." Poor Mrs. Moskowitz—she simply had no ear for sounds.

The class, made timid by Mrs. Moskowitz's disastrous effort, was silent.

"Corrections?" asked Mr. Parkhill again. "Come, come. Please don't be so—er—shy. Mr. Kaplan? No corrections?"

Mr. Kaplan smiled happily. "I'm positif is planty mistakes by Mitnick, but"—he grinned—"I'm still figgerink."

"Well, just give us the mistakes you jotted down." Mr. Parkhill nodded towards Mr. Kaplan's open notebook.

Mr. Kaplan shook his head pleasantly. "Not a tsingle mistake did I jotted don."

"But—" Mr. Parkhill smiled and walked over to Mr. Kaplan's desk. Mr. Kaplan held the notebook up. It was clear now what had taken so much of Mr. Kaplan's time and concentration. On the page he had printed in fine, strong letters:

Mistakes By Mitnick

By

H * Y * M * A * N   K * A * P * L * A * N

The rest of the page was blank.

Suddenly, Mr. Norman Bloom raised his hand. "It shouldn't be ½ after 7 and after 4," he said. "Like that is the figgers for size, like hats, or fractions—like 12½ ponds meat."

"Good!" said Mr. Parkhill. "That's a very good point. How should half-past seven and half-past four be written?"

"Saven-three-zero and four-three-zero," Mr. Bloom called off.

Mr. Parkhill erased "7" and "4." He wrote "730" and "430" in their places. "Like *this*, Mr. Bloom?" he asked, raising an eyebrow sententiously.

Mr. Kaplan had learned that whenever Mr. Parkhill raised an eyebrow sententiously the answer was "No." Mr. Kaplan shook his head vigorously, trying to catch Mr. Parkhill's eye.

"N-no," said Mr. Bloom, cautiously.

"Like *this*?" Mr. Parkhill made it "7-30" and "4-30." Mr. Kaplan, watching Mr. Parkhill's eyebrow like a hawk, cried "Ha!" and shook his head again.

"It still don' *look* good," said Mr. Bloom.

"Of course not!" cried Mr. Parkhill happily. "Well, like *this*?" He made it "7/30" and "4/30." His eyebrow was arched with absolute delight at the method he was using. ("The gradual elimination of incorrect alternatives.")

Mr. Bloom was silent.

"Wronk!" cried Mr. Kaplan with enthusiasm. "Plain wronk!"

The class looked up, impressed. Mr. Parkhill, let it be said, was impressed too.

"Yes, Mr. Kaplan. That *is* wrong." He had been keenly aware of the decision and accuracy of Mr. Kaplan's successive negations. "Tell the class which is the correct form." It was *splendid* to feel that Mr. Kaplan was making progress.

Mr. Kaplan's smile congealed into vacuity.

"I dunno," he said, the victim of his own strategy.

Mr. Parkhill felt distinctly let down. A case of knowing what was wrong, he thought, but not knowing what was *right*. A common failing. Without looking at Mr. Kaplan he inserted colons, making the numerals read "7:30" and "4:30."

"Now?" he asked. His tone was sententious, but a practiced eye would have seen that Mr. Parkhill's eyebrow was inert.

"Aha!" cried Mr. Kaplan. "Fine! Poifick! Dat's Hau Kay!"

It was, in its way, a minor redemption. Mr. Park-hill was glad, for Mr. Kaplan's sake.

"Correct, Mr. Kaplan. This mark is used in fig-ures, to indicate time, and in many other ways—as, for instance, to—er—introduce a long quotation, or after 'Dear Sir' in a letter."

Mr. Kaplan nodded, swathed in delight, a study in pride, agreement, and *noblesse oblige*. Mr. Park-hill placed a large, clear colon on the board.

"What do we call this mark?"

A nonplussed silence gripped the class.

"Semicolon?" asked Miss Mitnick tentatively.

"N-no, not quite. But that's close. Anyone?"

Up shot the hand of Hyman Kaplan.

"Again?" Mr. Parkhill said gaily. "Well, good for you! What *do* we call this mark of punctuation?"

"Two periods," said Mr. Kaplan, simply.

In a soft voice, and with his eyes on the black-board, Mr. Parkhill spoke. "No, Mr. Kaplan, I'm afraid not. . . . It's called the *colon*."

Then Mr. Parkhill went on, changing tenses, prep-ositions, dependent clauses; removing superfluous commas and adding necessary articles; making every correction, indeed, except the spelling of "head-ackes."

"I have left one mistake," he said at last. "A mistake in spelling. One word is obviously spelled incorrectly, and I should like someone in the class to correct it." Mr. Parkhill clung with undaunted faith to the "method of direct participation." That was the way Mr. Parkhill was. It was something in his makeup. "Please examine Miss Mitnick's composition carefully, everyone."

Eyes glazed, brows knit, foreheads moistened with perspiration as the beginners' grade of the American Night Preparatory School for Adults searched for truth. Miss Mitnick stared with an anxious look, as if wanting to wipe out her disgrace by being the first to locate the error. Mr. Bloom studied the composition on the board with feverish intensity. Mr. Kaplan smiled and murmured each word aloud to himself, to strengthen his analytic powers: "My—jop—is—beink—a—vaitress."

"Aha! 'Vaitress!' " he cried out. "Should be a 'v' in 'vaitress'!"

Mr. Parkhill shook his head severely. "No, Mr. Kaplan, decidedly not. The word is '*wait*ress,' not—er—'*vait*ress.' Just put the word 'wait,' from which 'waitress' comes, in front. A waitress is someone who *waits,* or waits on. 'Wait' is the first syllable; we spell it just as if it were alone."

"Oh."

Mr. Parkhill wasn't sure whether Mr. Kaplan looked sheepish or was just smiling less energetically.

"I think the word 'headackes' is in my composition wrong," said Miss Mitnick with dignity. "I wasn't sure about the spelling when I was writing it."

"Ufcawss!" Mr. Kaplan cried. " 'Hadakes' is wronk! Plain an' tsimple wronk!"

"That's what Miss Mitnick said," commented Mr. Parkhill caustically.

"Becawss she didn't spallink de void *just like as if it should be alone!*" Mr. Kaplan rushed on, exploiting the great principle he had learned. " 'Had-akes' —two voids! Spall like saparate, den put togadder— Like in 'vaitress' you puttink de 'vait' in front, so now you puttink de 'ackes' in back—an' de void must comm ot all right!"

This unexpected *tour de force* of analysis made Mr. Parkhill rather ashamed of his sarcasm a moment earlier. "Exactly!" he said. "The rule applies here in the same way. Spell the word as if it were two separate words; combine 'head' and 'aches' and you have 'headaches'!"

Mr. Kaplan beamed with joy. "Exactel vat I'm sayink, Mr. Pockheel! 'Hadakes' mit 'k' in de middle? Ha!" There was deep scorn in that "Ha!" "Is no 'k' in 'ackes' alone, so can't be a 'k' in 'hadakes'!"

By this time Mr. Parkhill was genuinely delighted with the inexorable logic which Mr. Kaplan was following.

"That's precisely the point. Come to the board and make the change, Mr. Kaplan."

Mr. Kaplan, ebullient, overjoyed, went to the board, took a piece of chalk, and scratched a firm line through the word Miss Mitnick had so lucklessly misspelled.

"No 'k'! Only two voids—'had' and 'akes.'"

Then, as the class watched with bated breath (Miss Mitnick lost in the torments of embarrassment), Mr. Kaplan printed, in letters three inches high, "H-E-A-D A-X-E."

For a long and pregnant moment Mr. Parkhill was as silent as the class, speechless before this orthographic triumph. Then he shook his head, slowly, with absolute finality. He felt that once again Mr. Kaplan had failed to fulfill an expectation which he had clearly aroused.

MR. K*A*P*L*A*N
AND THE MAGI

WHEN Mr. Parkhill saw that Miss Mitnick, Mr. Bloom, and Mr. Hyman Kaplan were absent, and that a strange excitement pervaded the beginners' grade, he realized that it was indeed the last night before the holidays and that Christmas was only a few days off. Each Christmas the classes in the American Night Preparatory School for Adults gave presents to their respective teachers. Mr. Parkhill, a veteran of many sentimental Yuletides, had come to know the procedure. That night, before the class session had begun, there must have been a hurried collection; a Gift Committee of three had been chosen; at this moment the Committee was probably in Mickey Goldstein's Arcade, bargaining feverishly, arguing about the appropriateness of a pair of pajamas or the color of a dozen linen handkerchiefs, debating whether Mr. Parkhill would prefer a pair of fleece-lined slippers to a set of mother-of-pearl cuff links.

"We shall concentrate on—er—spelling drill to-night," Mr. Parkhill announced.

The students smiled wisely, glanced at the three empty seats, exchanged knowing nods, and prepared for spelling drill. Miss Rochelle Goldberg giggled, then looked ashamed as Mrs. Rodriguez shot her a glare of reproval.

Mr. Parkhill always chose a spelling drill for the night before the Christmas vacation: it kept all the students busy simultaneously; it dampened the excitement of the occasion; above all, it kept him from the necessity of resorting to elaborate pedagogical efforts in order to hide his own embarrassment.

Mr. Parkhill called off the first words. Pens and pencils scratched, smiles died away, eyes grew serious, preoccupied, as the beginners' grade assaulted the spelling of "Banana . . . Romance . . . Groaning." Mr. Parkhill sighed. The class seemed incomplete without its star student, Miss Mitnick, and barren without its most remarkable one, Mr. Hyman Kaplan. Mr. Kaplan's most recent linguistic triumph had been a fervent speech extolling the D'Oyly Carte Company's performance of an operetta by two English gentlemen referred to as "Goldberg and Solomon."

"Charming . . . Horses . . . Float," Mr. Parkhill called off.

Mr. Parkhill's mind was not really on "Charming . . . Horses . . . Float." He could not help thinking of the momentous event which would take place that night. After the recess the students would come in with flushed faces and shining eyes. The Committee would be with them, and one member of the Committee, carrying an elaborately bound Christmas package, would be surrounded by several of the largest students in the class, who would try to hide the parcel from Mr. Parkhill's eyes. The class would come to order with uncommon rapidity. Then, just as Mr. Parkhill resumed the lesson, one member of the Committee would rise, apologize nervously for interrupting, place the package on Mr. Parkhill's desk, utter a few half-swallowed words, and rush back to his or her seat. Mr. Parkhill would say a few halting phrases of gratitude and surprise, everyone would smile and fidget uneasily, and the lesson would drag on, somehow, to the final and distant bell.

"*Ac*cept . . . *Ex*cept . . . Cucumber."

And as the students filed out after the final bell, they would cry "Merry Christmas, Happy New Year!" in joyous voices. The Committee would crowd around Mr. Parkhill with tremendous smiles to say that if the present wasn't *just right* in size or color (if it was something to wear) or in design (if it was something to use), Mr. Parkhill could exchange it. He didn't *have* to abide by the Committee's choice. He could exchange the present for *anything*. They would have arranged all that carefully with Mr. Mickey Goldstein himself.

That was the ritual, fixed and unchanging, of the last night of school before Christmas.

"Nervous . . . Goose . . . Violets."

The hand on the clock crawled around to eight. Mr. Parkhill could not keep his eyes off the three seats, so eloquent in their vacancy, which Miss Mitnick, Mr. Bloom, and Mr. Kaplan ordinarily graced with their presences. He could almost see these three in the last throes of decision in Mickey Goldstein's Arcade, harassed by the competitive attractions of gloves, neckties, an electric clock, a cane, spats, a "lifetime" fountain pen. Mr. Parkhill grew cold as he thought of a fountain pen. Three times already he had been presented with "lifetime" fountain pens, twice with "lifetime" pencils to match. Mr. Parkhill had exchanged these gifts: he had a fountain pen. Once he had chosen a woollen vest in-

stead; once a pair of mittens and a watch chain. Mr.
Parkhill hoped it wouldn't be a fountain pen. Or a
smoking jacket. He had never been able to understand how the Committee in '32 had decided upon a
smoking jacket. Mr. Parkhill did not smoke. He had
exchanged it for fur-lined gloves.

Just as Mr. Parkhill called off "Sardine . . . *Ex-*
quisite . . . Palace" the recess bell rang. The heads
of the students bobbed up as if propelled by a single
spring. There was a rush to the door, Mr. Sam
Pinsky well in the lead. Then, from the corridor,
their voices rose. Mr. Parkhill began to print
"Banana" on the blackboard, so that the students
could correct their own papers after recess. He tried
not to listen, but the voices in the corridor were like
the chatter of a flock of sparrows.

"Hollo, Mitnick!"

"Bloom, Bloom, vat is it?"

"So vat did you gat, Keplen? Tell!"

Mr. Parkhill could hear Miss Mitnick's shy "We
bought—" interrupted by Mr. Kaplan's stern cry,
"Mitnick! Don' say! Plizz, faller-students! Come
don mit de voices! Titcher vill awreddy hearink, you
hollerink so lod! Still! Order! Plizz!" There was
no question about it: Mr. Kaplan was born to com-
mand.

"Did you bought a Tsheaffer's Fontain Pan Sat, guarantee for de whole life, like *I* said?" one voice came through the door. A Sheaffer Fountain Pen Set, Guaranteed. That was Mrs. Moskowitz. Poor Mrs. Moskowitz, she showed so little imagination, even in her homework. "Moskovitz! Mein Gott!" the stentorian whisper of Mr. Kaplan soared through the air. "Vy you don' open op de door Titcher should *positivel* hear? Ha! Let's goink to odder and fromm de hall!"

The voices of the beginners' grade died away as they moved to the "odder and" of the corridor, like the chorus of "Aïda" vanishing into Egyptian wings.

Mr. Parkhill printed "Charming" and "Horses" on the board. For a moment he thought he heard Mrs. Moskowitz's voice repeating stubbornly, "Did —you—bought—a—Tsheaffer—Fontain—Pan— Sat—*Guarantee?*"

Mr. Parkhill began to say to himself, "Thank you, all of you. It's *just* what I wanted," again and again. One Christmas he hadn't said "It's just what I wanted" and poor Mrs. Oppenheimer, chairman of the Committee that year, had been hounded by the students' recriminations for a month.

It seemed an eternity before the recess bell rang again. The class came in *en masse,* and hastened to the seats from which they would view the impending spectacle. The air hummed with silence.

Mr. Parkhill was printing "Cucumber." He did not turn his face from the board as he said, "Er— please begin correcting your own spelling. I have printed most of the words on the board."

There was a low and heated whispering. "Stend op, Mitnick!" he heard Mr. Kaplan hiss. "You should stend op *too!*"

"The *whole* Committee," Mr. Bloom whispered. "Stand op!"

Apparently Miss Mitnick, a gazelle choked with embarrassment, did not have the fortitude to "stend op" with her colleagues.

"A fine raprezantitif *you'll* gonna make!" Mr. Kaplan hissed scornfully. "Isn't for *mine* sek I'm eskink, Mitnick. Plizz *stend op!*"

There was a confused, half-muted murmur, and the anguished voice of Miss Mitnick saying, "I *can't.*" Mr. Parkhill printed "Violets" on the board. Then there was a tense silence. And then the voice of Mr. Kaplan rose, firmly, clearly, with a decision and dignity which left no doubt as to its purpose.

"Podden me, Mr. Pockheel!"

It had come.

"Er—yes?" Mr. Parkhill turned to face the class.

Messrs. Bloom and Kaplan were standing side by side in front of Miss Mitnick's chair, holding between them a large, long package, wrapped in cellophane and tied with huge red ribbons. A pair of small hands touched the bottom of the box, listlessly. The owner of the hands, seated in the front row, was hidden by the box.

"De hends is Mitnick," Mr. Kaplan said apologetically.

Mr. Parkhill gazed at the tableau. It was touching.

"Er—yes?" he said again feebly, as if he had forgotten his lines and was repeating his cue.

"Hau Kay!" Mr. Kaplan whispered to his confreres. The hands disappeared behind the package. Mr. Kaplan and Mr. Bloom strode to the platform with the box. Mr. Kaplan was beaming, his smile rapturous, exalted. They placed the package on Mr. Parkhill's desk, Mr. Bloom dropped back a few paces, and Mr. Kaplan said, "Mr. Pockheel! Is mine beeg honor, becawss I'm Chairman fromm de Buyink an' Deliverink to You a Prazent Committee, to givink to you dis fine peckitch."

Mr. Parkhill was about to stammer, "Oh, thank

you," when Mr. Kaplan added hastily, "Also I'll sayink a few voids."

Mr. Kaplan took an envelope out of his pocket. He whispered loudly, "Mitnick, *you still got time to comm op mit de Committee*," but Miss Mitnick only blushed furiously and lowered her eyes. Mr. Kaplan sighed, straightened the envelope, smiled proudly at Mr. Parkhill, and read.

"Dear Titcher—dat's de beginnink. Ve stendink on de adge fromm a beeg holiday." He cleared his throat. "Ufcawss is all kinds holidays in U. S. A. Holidays for politic, for religious, an' *plain* holidays. In Fabrary, ve got Judge Vashington's boitday, a *fine* holiday. Also Abram Lincohen's. In May ve got Memorable Day, for dad soldiers. In July comms, netcheral, Fort July. Also ve have Labor Day, Denksgivink, for de Peelgrims, an' for de feenish fromm de Voild Var, *Armistress* Day."

Mr. Parkhill played with a piece of chalk nervously.

"But arond dis time year ve have a *difference* kind holiday, a spacial, movvellous time. Dat's called —Chrissmas."

Mr. Parkhill put the chalk down.

"All hover de voild," Mr. Kaplan mused, "is

pipple celebraking dis vunderful time. Becawss for som pipple is Chrissmas like for *odder* pipple is Passover. Or Chanukah, batter. De most fine, de most beauriful, de most *secret* holiday fromm de whole bunch!"

(" 'Sacred,' Mr. Kaplan, 'sacred,' " Mr. Parkhill thought, ever the pedagogue.)

"Ven ve valkink don de stritt an' is snow on de floor an' all kinds tarrible cold!" Mr. Kaplan's hand leaped up dramatically, like a flame. "Ven ve see in de vindows trees mit rad an' grin laktric lights boinink! Ven is de time for tellink de fancy-tales abot Sandy Claws commink fromm Naut Pole on rain-enimals, an' climbink don de jiminies mit *stockings* for all de leetle kits! Ven ve hearink abot de beauri-ful toughts of de Tree Vise Guys who vere follerink a star fromm de dasert! Ven pipple sayink, 'Oh, Mary Chrissmas! Oh, Heppy Noo Yiss! Oh, bast regotts!' Den ve *all* got a varm fillink in de heart for all humanity vhich should be brodders!"

Mr. Feigenbaum nodded philosophically at this profound thought; Mr. Kaplan, pleased, nodded back.

"*You* got de fillink, Mr. Pockheel. *I* got de fillink, dat's no qvastion abot! Bloom, Pinsky, Caravello,

Schneiderman, even Mitnick"—Mr. Kaplan was
punishing Miss Mitnick tenfold for her perfidy—
"got de fillink! An' vat is it?" There was a momentous pause. "De Chrissmas Spirits!"

(" 'Spir*it*,' Mr. Kaplan, 'spir*it*,' " the voice of Mr.
Parkhill's conscience said.)

"Now I'll givink de prazent," Mr. Kaplan announced subtly. Mr. Bloom shifted his weight. "Becawss you a foist-cless titcher, Mr. Pockheel, an'
learn abot gremmer an' spallink an' de hoddest pots
pernonciation—ve know is a planty hod jop mit soch
students—so ve fill you should havink a sample
fromm our—fromm our—" Mr. Kaplan turned
the envelope over hastily—"aha! Fromm our santi-
mental!"

Mr. Parkhill stared at the long package and the
huge red ribbons.

"Fromm de cless, to our lovely Mr. Pockheel!"

Mr. Parkhill started. "Er—?" he asked involun-
tarily.

"Fromm de cless, to our lovely Mr. Pockheel!"
Mr. Kaplan repeated with pride.

(" '*Beloved*,' Mr. Kaplan, '*beloved*.' ")

A hush had fallen over the room. Mr. Kaplan, his
eyes bright with joy, waited for Mr. Parkhill to take

up the ritual. Mr. Parkhill tried to say, "Thank you, Mr. Kaplan," but the phrase seemed meaningless, so big, so ungainly, that it could not get through his throat. Without a word Mr. Parkhill began to open the package. He slid the big red ribbons off. He broke the tissue paper inside. For some reason his vision was blurred and it took him a moment to identify the present. It was a smoking jacket. It was black and gold, and a dragon with a green tongue was embroidered on the breast pocket.

"Horyantal style," Mr. Kaplan whispered delicately.

Mr. Parkhill nodded. The air trembled with the tension. Miss Mitnick looked as if she were ready to cry. Mr. Bloom peered intently over Mr. Kaplan's shoulder. Mrs. Moskowitz sat entranced, sighing with behemothian gasps. She looked as if she were at her daughter's wedding.

"Thank you," Mr. Parkhill stammered at last. "Thank you, all of you."

Mr. Bloom said, "Hold it op everyone should see."

Mr. Kaplan turned on Mr. Bloom with an icy look. "*I'm* de chairman!" he hissed.

"I—er—I can't tell you how much I appreciate

your kindness," Mr. Parkhill said without lifting his eyes.

Mr. Kaplan smiled. "So now you'll plizz hold op de prazent. Plizz."

Mr. Parkhill took the smoking jacket out of the box and held it up for all to see. There were gasps— "Oh!"s and "Ah!"s and Mr. Kaplan's own ecstatic "My! Is beauriful!" The green tongue on the dragon seemed alive.

"Maybe ve made a mistake," Mr. Kaplan said hastily. "Maybe you don' smoke—dat's how *Mitnick* tought." The scorn dripped. "But I said, 'Ufcawss is Titcher smokink! Not in de cless, netcheral. At home! At least a *pipe!*'"

"No, no, you didn't make a mistake. It's—it's *just* what I wanted!"

The great smile on Mr. Kaplan's face became dazzling. "Hooray! Vear in de bast fromm helt!" he cried impetuously. "Mary Chrissmas! Heppy Noo Yiss! You should have a *hondert* more!"

This was the signal for a chorus of acclaim. "Mary Chrissmas!" "Wear in best of health!" "Happy New Year!" Miss Schneiderman burst into applause, followed by Mr. Scymzak and Mr. Weinstein. Miss Caravello, carried away by all the excitement, uttered

some felicitations in rapid Italian. Mrs. Moskowitz
sighed once more and said, "Soch a *sveet* ceremonia."
Miss Mitnick smiled feebly, blushing, and twisted
her handkerchief.

The ceremony was over. Mr. Parkhill began to put
the smoking jacket back into the box with fumbling
hands. Mr. Bloom marched back to his seat. But
Mr. Kaplan stepped a little closer to the desk. The
smile had congealed on Mr. Kaplan's face. It was
poignant and profoundly earnest.

"Er—thank you, Mr. Kaplan," Mr. Parkhill said
gently.

Mr. Kaplan shuffled his feet, looking at the floor.
For the first time since Mr. Parkhill had known him,
Mr. Kaplan seemed to be embarrassed. Then, just as
he turned to rush back to his seat, Mr. Kaplan
whispered, so softly that no ears but Mr. Parkhill's
heard it, "Maybe de spitch I rad vas too *formmal*.
But avery void I said—it came fromm *bolow mine
heart!*"

Mr. Parkhill felt that, for all his weird, unortho-
dox English, Mr. Kaplan had spoken with the
tongues of the Magi.

MR. K*A*P*L*A*N'S
WHITE BANNER

IT was only logical that, having drilled the class before the holidays on the writing of personal letters, Mr. Parkhill should now take up the business form with the beginners' grade. Business letters, indeed, might be even more practical from the students' point of view. They might want to apply for a job, or answer an advertisement, or things of that sort.

"The general structure of the business letter follows that of the personal letter," Mr. Parkhill had said. "It, too, requires the address, the date, a salutation, a final greeting or 'complimentary close.'" Then he had gone on to explain that the business letter was more formal in mood and content; that the address of the person or company to whom you were writing had to be included in the form of the letter itself, on the left-hand side, above the salutation; that both the salutation and final greeting were formalized: "Dear Sir," "Dear Sirs," or "Gentlemen," and "Yours truly," "Yours very truly," "Very truly yours." Mr. Parkhill was a conscientious teacher and.

aware of the queer things some of the students had
done with previous exercises, he was careful to introduce the beginners' grade to business letters with particular care.

All had gone well—very well. So much had Mr.
Parkhill been pleased by his success that, for home-
work, he had assigned a composition entitled "A
Short Business Letter."

And now the students were presenting their homework on the blackboard for class analysis. Mrs.
Tomasic, anticipating some halcyon day in the future, was applying for a position as private secretary
to the President of the Good English Club. Mr.
George Weinstein was ordering "a dozen assoted
colors sox size 12 silk" from a well-known department store. Mr. Norman Bloom, ever the soul of
business, was inscribing a polite but firm note remind-
ing "S. Levin—Inc.—Jobbers" that they still owed
him $17.75 for merchandise taken "on assignment."
Miss Schneiderman described a hat, coat, and "pair
gloffs" she wished deliverd "C.O.T." Mr. Hyman
Kaplan was copying his letter on the blackboard in
the right-hand corner of the room, near the door.
There was a serenity in Mr. Kaplan's ubiquitous
smile as he put the finishing touches to his creation.
This night there was something luminous about

that smile. Mr. Parkhill, always uneasy about the form Mr. Kaplan's genius might give to any assignment, found himself reading Mr. Kaplan's letter with unconscious curiosity and quite conscious anxiety. This was the letter Mr. Kaplan had written:

Bus. Let.

459 E. 3. Street
New York
Janu. 8

JOSEPH MANDELBAUM
A-1 Furniture Comp. N.Y.

DEAR SIR MANDELBAUM—

Sarah and me want to buy refrigimator. Sarah wants bad. Always she is saying "Hymie, the eyes-box is terrible. Leeking." Is true. So I answer "Sarah, by me is O.K. refrigimator."

Because you are in furniture so I'm writing about. How much will cost refrigimator? Is axpensif, maybe by you is more cheap a little. But it *must not* have short circus. If your eye falls on a bargain please pick it up.

Very Truly Your Customer

H * Y * M * A * N   K * A * P * L * A * N

(Address on Top)

Best regards Sarah and me.

Affectionately,

H * Y * M * I * E

Mr. Parkhill frowned several times during his reading of this document, sighed when he had finished his examination of it, and resigned himself to another tortuous excursion into the strange linguistic universe of his most remarkable student. As for Mr. Kaplan, he reread his handiwork several times lovingly, his eyes half-closed in what was supposed to be a self-critical attitude. He kept shaking his head happily as he read, smiling, as if delighted by the miracle of what he had brought into being. Mr. Kaplan was an appreciative soul.

When the last student had finished, Mr. Parkhill said quickly, "I think we'll take your composition *first*, Mr. Kaplan." He wasn't quite sure why he had said that. Generally he started with the exercise in the *left*-hand corner of the blackboard.

"Me *foist?*" asked Mr. Kaplan.

"Er—yes." Mr. Parkhill almost wavered at the last minute.

Mr. Kaplan's smile widened. "My!" he said, getting up from his seat. "Is awreddy *foist* I'm makink rasitations!" By the time he reached the blackboard his smile had become positively celestial.

Mr. Kaplan faced the class, as if it were an exercise in Recitation and Speech rather than composition.

"Ladies an' gantleman," he began, "in dis lasson I falt a fonny kind problem. A problem abot how—"

"Er—Mr. Kaplan," Mr. Parkhill broke in, "please *read* your letter."

Only Mr. Kaplan's delight in being first carried him over this cruel frustration. "Podden me," he said softly. He began to read the letter. " 'Dear Sir Mendelbum.' " He read slowly, with dignity, with feeling. His smile struggled between pride and modesty. When he came to the last words, there was a tinge of melancholy in his voice. " 'Affectionately, Hymie.' " Mr. Kaplan sighed. "Dat's de and."

"Mr. Kaplan," began Mr. Parkhill cautiously, "do you think that's strictly a *business* letter?"

Mr. Kaplan considered this challenge by closing his eyes and whispering to himself. "Business ladder? *Streectly* business ladder? Is?"

Mr. Parkhill waited. The years had taught Mr. Parkhill patience.

"It's *abot* business," suggested Mr. Kaplan tentatively.

Mr. Parkhill shook his head. "But the content, Mr. Kaplan. The tone. The final—er—well—" Mr. Parkhill caught *himself* on the verge of an oration.

"I'll let the class begin the corrections. There are *many* mistakes, Mr. Kaplan."

Mr. Kaplan's grave nod indicated that even the wisest of men knew what it was to err.

"Corrections, class. First, let us consider the basic question. Is this a business letter?"

The hand of Rose Mitnick went up with a menacing resolution. When the work of Mr. Kaplan was under consideration, Miss Mitnick functioned with devastating efficiency.

"I think this isn't," she said. "Because in business letter you don't tell your wife's *first* name. And you don't send 'best regards.' All that's for *personal* letters like we had before."

"An' vat if I vanted to wride a *poisonal* business ladder?" asked Mr. Kaplan with diabolic logic.

Miss Mitnick paid no attention to this casuistry. "It's wrong to give family facts in business letter," she insisted. "It's no business from the company what is a wife saying to a husband."

"Aha!" cried Mr. Kaplan. "Mitnick, you too ax-cited. You forgeddink to *who* is dis ladder!"

Mr. Parkhill cleared his throat. "Er—Mr. Kaplan, Miss Mitnick is quite right. One doesn't discuss personal or family details, or give one's wife's first

name, in a business letter—which is, after all, to a
stranger."

Mr. Kaplan waited until the last echo of Mr.
Parkhill's voice had died away. Then, when the classroom was very quiet, he spoke. "Mendelbum," he
said, "is mine oncle."

There was a collective gasp. Miss Mitnick flushed.
Mr. Marcus' eyes opened very wide. Mrs. Friedman
blinked blankly.

"But, Mr. Kaplan," said Mr. Parkhill quickly,
realizing that in such a mood there were no limits to
Mr. Kaplan's audacity, "if the letter *is* addressed to
your uncle"—he pronounced "uncle" suspiciously,
but Mr. Kaplan's firm nod convinced him that there
was no subterfuge here—"then it shouldn't be a business letter in the first place!"

To this Miss Mitnick nodded, with hope.

"Dat pozzled me, too," said Mr. Kaplan graciously. "An' dat's vy I vas goink to axplain abot de
fonny kind problem I falt, in de few voids before
I rad de ladder." His tone was one of righteousness.
"I figgered: buyink a refrigima—"

"Refrig*erator*! 'R' not 'm.' "

"Buyink a refrig*erator* is business. Also de axer-
cise you givink for homevork is abot business. So I

must kipp in business *atmosvere*. So in de foist pot I wrote mine oncle a real business ladder—cold, formmal. You know, stock-op!" Mr. Kaplan wrinkled his nose into a pictorialization of "stock-op." "But den, by de and, I falt is awreddy time to have mit family fillink. Becawss *is*, efter all, mine oncle. So I put don 'Affectionately, Hymie.' "

"And is 'Affectionately' right for a business letter?" asked Miss Mitnick, trying to conceal the triumph in her voice.

"It's *spalled* right!" Mr. Kaplan cried with feeling.

Mr. Parkhill felt old and weary; he began to realize the heights yet to be scaled. "Mr. Kaplan," he said softly, "we are not concerned with the spelling of 'affectionately' at the moment. 'Affectionately' is *not* proper in a business letter, nor is 'Very truly yours' in a personal letter." He spent a few minutes analyzing the impasse. "You cannot combine the two forms, Mr. Kaplan. Either you write a business letter *or* a personal letter." He suggested that in the future Mr. Kaplan write personal letters to his uncle, but choose absolute strangers for his business communications. "Let us go on with the corrections, please."

Mr. Bloom's hand went up.

"Mistakes is terrible," he said. "Where's the address from the company? How is abbreviated 'Company'? Where's colon or comma after 'Dear Sir'? And 'Dear Sir Mandelbaum'! What kind combination is this? Is maybe Mr. Kaplan's uncle in English House Lords?"

Mr. Kaplan smiled bravely through this fusillade. Even the sarcasm about his titled lineage did no perceptible damage to that smile.

" 'Sarah and me' should be 'Sarah and I,' " Mr. Bloom went on. "And 'eyes-box'! Phooey! I-c-e means 'ice'; e-y-e-s means 'eyes.' One is for seeing, the other for freezing!"

Mr. Bloom was in faultless form. The class listened breathlessly to his dissection of Mr. Kaplan's business letter. His recitation filled them with confidence. When he finished, a forest of hands went up. With new courage the beginners' grade leaped into the critical fray. It was pointed out that "leaking" was spelled wrong, and "expensive." Mr. Pinsky remarked pointedly that there should be no capitals after "Very" in "Very truly" and cast doubts on the legitimacy of "Very Truly Your Customer." Miss Caravello suggested that Mr. Mandelbaum

might be wise enough to read Mr. Kaplan's address
without being told where to look for it, in the phrase
"Address on Top." Even Mrs. Moskowitz, simple,
uninspired Mrs. Moskowitz, added her bit to the au-
topsy.

"I only know vun ting," she said. "I know vat is
a circus. Dat's mit hanimals, clons, tricks, horses. An'
you ken't put a circus in icebox—even a *short
circus*!"

"You don' know abot laktric!" cried Mr. Kaplan,
desperate to strike back at this united front. "Ufcawss, you a voman."

"Laktric—gas—even *candles!*" retorted Mrs.
Moskowitz. "Circus ken't go in icebox!"

"Maybe de kind *you* minn," said Mr. Kaplan
hotly. "But in laktricity is alvays denger havink short
coicus. Becawss—"

Mr. Parkhill intervened, conscious that here was
the making of a feud to take its place beside the
Mitnick-Kaplan *affaire*. "You don't mean 'short
circus,' Mr. Kaplan. You mean 'short cir*cuit!*'
C-i-r-c-u-i-t."

From the expression on Mr. Kaplan's face it was
clear that even this approximation to "circus" was a
victory for him and a rebuff to Mrs. Moskowitz and

the forces she had, for the moment, led into battle.

"Another mistake," said Miss Mitnick suddenly. There was a glow in her cheeks; evidently Miss Mitnick had discovered something very important. Mr. Kaplan's eyes turned to narrow slits. "In the letter is: 'If your eye falls on a bargain please pick it up.' " Miss Mitnick read the sentence slowly. " 'If your *eye* falls on a bargain pick *it* up?' "

The class burst into laughter. It was a masterly stroke. Everyone laughed. Even Mr. Parkhill, feeling a bit sorry for Mr. Kaplan, permitted himself a dignified smile.

And suddenly Mr. Kaplan joined in the merriment. He didn't laugh; he merely smiled. But his smile was grandiose, invincible, cosmic.

"An' vat's wronk dere, plizz?" he asked, his tone the epitome of confidence.

Mr. Bloom should have known that he was treading on ground mined with dynamite. But so complete had been the rout of Hyman Kaplan that Mr. Bloom threw caution to the winds. "Miss Mitnick's right! 'If your *eye* falls on a bargain please pick *it* up?' Som English, Mr. Kaplan!"

Then Mr. Kaplan struck.

"Mine oncle," he said, "has a gless eye."

The effect was incredible. The laughter came to a convulsive stop. Mr. Bloom's mouth fell open. Miss Mitnick dropped her pencil. Mrs. Moskowitz looked at Mr. Kaplan as if she had seen a vision; she wondered how she had dared criticize such a man. And Mr. Kaplan's smile was that of a child, deep in some lovely and imperishable sleep. He was like a man who had redeemed himself, a man whose honor, unsmirched, was before him like a dazzling banner.

O K*A*P*L*A*N!
MY K*A*P*L*A*N!

MR. PARKHILL was not surprised when the first
three students to participate in Recitation and Speech
practice delivered eloquent orations on "Abraham
Lincoln," "Little George and the Sherry Tree," and
"Wonderful U. S.," respectively. For the activities
of the month of February had injected a patriotic
fervor into the beginners' grade, an *amor patriae*
which would last well into March. There was a
simple enough reason for this phenomenon: Mr.
Robinson, principal of the school, did not allow
either Lincoln's or Washington's Birthday to pass
without appropriate ceremonies. On each occasion the
whole student body would crowd into Franklin Hall,
the largest of the five rooms occupied by the school,
to commemorate the nativity of one of the two great
Americans.

At the Lincoln assembly, Mr. Robinson always
gave a long eulogy entitled "The Great Emanicipa-
tor." ("His name is inscribed on the immortal roll

of history, in flaming letters of eternal gold!")
A "prize" student from the graduating class deliv-
ered a carefully corrected speech on "Lincoln and the
Civil War"—a rather short speech. Then Miss
Higby recited "O Captain! My Captain!" to an au-
dience which listened with reverently bated breath.

For the Washington convocation, the order of
things was much the same. Mr. Robinson's address
was entitled "The Father of His Country." ("First
in war, first in peace, and first in the hearts of his
countrymen—his name burns in the hearts of true
Americans, each letter a glowing ember, a symbol of
his glorious achievement!") The prize student's
speech was on "Washington and the American Revo-
lution." And Miss Higby recited "My Country, 'Tis
of Thee." (Miss Higby often remarked that it was a
sad commentary on our native bards that there was
no poem as *perfectly* appropriate for Washington
as "O Captain! My Captain!" was for Lincoln.)

The result of these patriotic rites was that for
weeks afterward, each year, the faculty would be
deluged with compositions on Lincoln or Washington, speeches on Washington or Lincoln, even little
poems on Lincoln or Washington. Night after night,
the classrooms echoed with the hallowed phrases

"1776," "Father of His Country," "The Great Emancipator," "The Civil War," "Honest Abe," "Valley Forge." Mr. Parkhill found it a nerve-sapping ordeal. He thought of this annual period as "the Ides of February and March."

"I will spik ona Garibaldi," announced Miss Caravello, the fourth student to face the class.

Mr. Parkhill felt a surge of gratitude within him. It was, however, short-lived.

"Garibaldi—joosta lak Washington! Firsta da war, firsta da peace, firsta da heartsa da country-mens!"

In the middle of the front row, Mr. Hyman Kaplan printed his name aimlessly for the dozenth time on a large sheet of foolscap, and sighed. Mr. Kaplan had been sighing, quite audibly, throughout each of the successive historico-patriotic declamations. Mr. Parkhill felt a distinct sense of comradeship with Mr. Kaplan.

"Hisa name burns, lak Mist' Principal say. Da 'g,' da 'a,' da 'r,' da 'i' . . ." Miss Caravello articulated the letters with gusto. Mr. Norman Bloom sharpened his pencil. Miss Schneiderman stared into space, vacantly. Mrs. Moskowitz rounded out the latest of a lengthy series of yawns. Mr. Parkhill frowned.

"Hooray Washington! Viva Garibaldi!"

In a fine Latin flush, Miss Caravello resumed her seat. Mr. Kaplan sighed again, rather more publicly. E * N * N * U * I was stamped on Mr. Kaplan's features.

"Corrections, please," Mr. Parkhill announced, trying to be as cheery as possible.

The zest of competition animated the class for a few brief moments. Miss Mitnick began the discussion, commenting on Miss Caravello's failure to distinguish between the past and present tenses of verbs, and her habit of affixing mellifluous "a"s to prosaic Anglo-Saxon words. Mr. Pinsky suggested, with a certain impatience, that it was "foist *in* war, foist *in* peace, foist *in* the hots his countryman."

"How you can comparink a Judge Vashington mit a Gary Baldy?" Mr. Kaplan remarked with icy scorn. "Ha!"

Mr. Parkhill quickly spread oil on the troubled nationalistic waters. To avoid an open clash (Miss Caravello had long ago allied herself with the Mitnick forces in the Kaplan-Mitnick vendetta), and in an effort to introduce a more stimulating note into Recitation and Speech, Mr. Parkhill said, "Er—suppose *you* speak next, Mr. Kaplan." Mr. Parkhill had learned to respect the catalytic effect of Mr. Kaplan's performances, oral or written.

Mr. Kaplan's ever-incipient smile burst into full bloom. He advanced to the front of the room, stuffing crayons into his pocket. Then he buttoned his coat with delicate propriety, made a little bow to Mr. Parkhill, and began, "Ladies an' gantleman, faller-students, an' Mr. Pockheel." He paused for the very fraction of a moment, as if permitting the class to steel itself; then, in a dramatic voice, he cried, "JUDGE VASHINGTON, ABRAM LINCOHEN, AN' JAKE POPPER!"

The class was galvanized out of its lassitude. Other students, less adventurous students, might undertake comments on Lincoln *or* Washington, but only Mr. Kaplan had the vision and the fortitude to encompass Lincoln *and* Washington—to say nothing of "Jake Popper."

"Er—Mr. Kaplan," suggested Mr. Parkhill anxiously. "It's *George W*ashington, not 'Judge.' And Abra*ham* Lin*coln*, not 'Ab*ram* Lin*cohen.*' Please try it again." (Mr. Parkhill could think of nothing relevant to say in regard to "Jake Popper.")

"*JAW*DGE VASHINGTON, ABRA*HAM* LIN*COLLEN*, AN'

JAKE POPPER!" Mr. Kaplan repeated, with renewed ardor. "Is dat right, Mr. Pockheel?"

Mr. Parkhill decided it might be best to let well enough alone. "It's—er—*better*."

"Hau Kay! So foist abot Jawdge Vashington. He vas a fine man. Ectually Fodder fromm His Contry, like dey say. Ve hoid awreddy, fromm planty students, all abot his movvellous didds. How, by beink even a leetle boy, he chopped don de cherries so he could enswer, 'I cannot tell lies, Papa. I did it mit mine leetle hatchik!' But ve shouldn't forgat dat Vashington vas a beeg ravolutionist! He vas fightink for Friddom, against de Kink Ingland, Kink Jawdge Number Tree, dat tarrible autocrap who—"

" 'Auto*crat*'!" Mr. Parkhill put in, but too late.

"—who vas puddink stemps on *tea* even, so it tasted bed, an' Jawdge Vashington trew de tea in Boston Hobber, drassed op like a Hindian. So vas de Ravolution!"

The class, Mr. Parkhill could not help observing, hung on Mr. Kaplan's every word, entranced by his historiography.

"Jawdge Vashington vas a hero. A foist-cless hero! In de meedle de coldest vedder he crossed de ice in a leetle boat, he should cetch de Bridish an' de missionaries—"

" '*Mercen*aries,' Mr. Kaplan, '*mer*cenaries'!"

"—foolink arond, not mit deir minds on de var!" Mr. Kaplan, having finished the sentence, said, "Podden me, '*Moisinaries*' I mant!" and, with scarcely a break in his stride, continued. "So efter de Ravolution de pipple said, 'Jawdge Vashington, you our hero an' lidder! Ve elactink you Prazident!' So he vas elacted Prazident U. S.—anonymously!"

Mr. Parkhill's " 'Unaminously!' " was lost in Mr. Kaplan's next words.

"An' like Mr. Robinson said, 'In Vashington's name is itch ladder like a coal, boinink ot his gloryous achivmants!' "

Mr. Kaplan ended the peroration with a joyous sweep of the arm.

"Mr. Kaplan!" Mr. Parkhill took the occasion to interrupt firmly. "You *must* speak more slowly, and —er—more carefully. You are making too many mistakes, far too many. It is *very* difficult to correct your English." Mr. Parkhill was aware that "Abraham Lincollen an' Jake Popper" were still to come.

Mr. Kaplan's face fell as he recognized the necessity of smothering the divine fire which flamed within

him. "I'll try mine bast," he said. In a gentler mood,
he continued. "Vell, I said a lot fine tings abot
Jawdge Vashington. But enyho, is Abraham Lincollen more *close* to me. Dat Abraham Lincollen! Vat
a sveet man. Vat a fine cherecter. Vat a hot—like
gold! Look!" Mr. Kaplan pointed dramatically to
the lithograph of the Great Emancipator which hung
on the back wall; the heads of the students turned.
"Look on his face! Look his ice, so sad mit fillink.
Look his mot, so full goodness. Look de high forehat
—dat's showink smotness, *brains!*" Mr. Kaplan's in-
vidious glance toward Miss Caravello left no doubt
that this high quality was missing in "Gary Baldy."
"Look de honest axpression! I esk, is it a *vunder*
dey vas callink him 'Honest Abie'?"

" 'Honest Abe!' " Mr. Parkhill exclaimed with
some desperation, but Mr. Kaplan, carried away by
the full, rich sweep of his passion, had soared on.

"No, it's no vunder. He vas a poor boy, a vood-
chopper, a rail-splinter like dey say. But he made de
Tsivil Var! Oh my, den vas tarrible times! Shoodink,
killink, de Naut Site U. S. A. aganst de Sot Site
U. S. A. Black neegers aganst vhite, brodder fightink
brodder, de Blues mit de Grays. An' who von? *Who?*
Ha! Abraham Lincollen von, netcherally! So he

made de neegers should be like vhite. Ufcawss, Lincollen didn't change de *collars*," Mr. Kaplan foot-
noted with scholarly discretion. "Dey vas still *black*.
But *free* black, not slafe black. Den"—Mr. Kaplan's
voice took on a pontifical note—"Lincollen gave ot
de Mancipation Prockilmation. Dat vas, dat all men
are born an' created *in de same vay!* So he vas
killed."

Exhausted by this mighty passage, Mr. Kaplan
paused. Mrs. Moskowitz chose the opportunity to
force down a yawn.

"Vell, vat's got all dis to do mit Jake Popper?"
Mr. Kaplan asked suddenly. He had taken the question out of the very mouths of Miss Mitnick, Mr.
Bloom, *et al.* It was a triumph of prescience. "Vell,
Jake Popper vas also a fine man, mit a hot like gold.
Ve called him 'Honest Jake.' Ufcawss, Jake Popper
vasn't a beeg soldier; he didn't make Velley Fudges
or free slafes. Jake Popper had a dalicatessen store."
(The modest shrug which accompanied this sentence
made it live and breathe: "Jake Popper had a dalicatessen store.") "An' in his store could even poor
pipple mitout money, alvays gat somting to eat—if
dey vas honest. Jake Popper did a tremandous beeg
business—on cradit. An' averybody loved him.

"Vun day vas 'Honest Jake' fillink bed. He had hot an' cold vaves on de body by de same time; vat ve call a fivver. So averybody said, 'Jake, lay don in bad, rast.' But did Jake Popper lay don in bad, rast? No! He stayed in store, day an' night. He said, 'I got to tink abot mine *customers!*' Dat's de kind high sanse *duty* he had!"

Whether from throat strain or emotion, a husky tone crept into Mr. Kaplan's voice at this point.

"Den de doctor came an' said, 'Popper, you got bronxitis!' So Jake vent in bad. An' he got voise an' voise. So de doctor insulted odder doctors—"

" '*Con*sulted' other—"

"—an' dey took him in Mont Sinai Hospital. He had double demonia! So dere vas spacial noises, an' fromm all kinds maditzins de bast, an' an oxen tant, he should be able to breed. Even blood confusions dey gave him!"

" '*Trans*fusions,' Mr. Kaplan!" It was no use. Mr. Kaplan, like a spirited steed, was far ahead.

"An' dey shot him in de arm, he should fallink aslip. Dey gave him *epidemics*." Mr. Parkhill estimated his speed and made no protest. "An' efter a vhile, 'Honest Jake' Popper pest avay."

Mr. Kaplan's face was bathed in reverence, suffused with a lofty dignity. Mrs. Moskowitz yawned no more; she was shaking her head sadly, back and forth, back and forth. (Mrs. Moskowitz wore her heart on her sleeve.)

"So in Jake Popper's honor I made dis leettle spitch. An' I vant also to say for him somting like 'O Ceptin! My Ceptin!'—dat Miss Higby said abot Abraham Lincollen. I got fromm her de voids." Mr. Kaplan took a piece of paper out of an inner vest pocket, drew his head up high, and, as Mr. Parkhill held his breath, read:

> "O hot! hot! hot!
> O de bliddink drops rad!
> Dere on de dack
> Jake Popper lies,
> Fallink cold an' dad!"

Celestial wings fluttered over the beginners' grade of the American Night Preparatory School for Adults, whispering of the grandeur that was Popper.

"Isn't dat beauriful?" Mr. Kaplan mused softly, with the detachment of the true artist. "My!"

Mr. Parkhill was just about to call for corrections when Mr. Kaplan said, "Vun ting more I should say, so de cless shouldn't fill *too* bed abot Jake Popper. It's awreddy nine yiss since he pest avay!"

Mrs. Moskowitz shot Mr. Kaplan a furious look: her tender emotions had been cruelly exploited.

"An' *I* didn't go to de funeral!" On this strange note, Mr. Kaplan took his seat.

The class hummed, protesting against this anticlimax which left so much to the imagination.

"*Why you didn't?*" cried Mr. Bloom, with a knowing nod to the Misses Mitnick and Caravello.

Mr. Kaplan's face was a study in sufferance. "Becawss de funeral vas in de meedle of de veek," he sighed. "An' I said to minesalf, 'Keplen, you in America, so tink like de *Americans* tink!' So I tought, an' I didn't go. Becawss I tought of dat *dip* American idea, '*Business bafore pleasure!*' "

MR. K*A*P*L*A*N'S
SO-AND-SO

THE March rain slithered across the windows. It was a nasty night, a night of wet feet, drab spirits, and head colds. Mr. Parkhill, indeed, *had* a head cold. He was at home, indisposed, and a young substitute teacher, bubbling with the courage of a year and a half of practice teaching, was at the desk in front of the beginners' grade. The young man could tell, by the way the students received the sad news of Mr. Parkhill's indisposition, that they really liked him and were worried by his absence. This filled the young substitute with pride in his calling.

"Is maybe Mr. Pockheel *seryous* seeck?" asked a pleasant-looking gentleman in the front row, center.

"No, I'm sure not. He'll be back with you Monday night, Mr.—?"

"Hymen Keplen," the man with the pleasant face said. His smile was either profoundly modest or completely automatic.

"—Mr. Kaplan."

"Denks Gott isn't seryous awreddy," sighed Mr. Kaplan with relief. Many other students sighed with relief, too; the collective sighs were like a choral "Amen!" "Dat soitinly takes a beeg load off!"

"You mean 'That takes a load off my mind'!" Mr. Parkhill's substitute corrected quickly. Nothing escaped this young man.

"A load off mine *mind?*" Mr. Kaplan repeated softly. He thought this over for a moment, nodded, and then said, "An' off mine *hot* also."

The young man saw at once that this Mr. Kaplan had a subtle mind. (Had he known that only last week Mr. Kaplan had said "For eatink smashed potatoes I am usink a knife an' fog!" he would have concluded that Mr. Kaplan had a *remarkable* mind.)

"Well, let us begin tonight's lesson. Mr. Parkhill suggested that we—"

"Podden me, Titcher." It was Mr. Kaplan again, Mr. Kaplan with an apologetic smile. "Can ve know plizz *your* name?"

The young man laughed boyishly. "Well, pardon me! How stupid of me. Of course. My name is Jennings."

From the look on Mr. Kaplan's face, the name

might have been that of a Chinaman. "Channink?" he asked, incredulously.

"No, *Jennings.* J-e-n-n-i-n-g-s." The young man wrote the characters on the board with undismayed fingers.

"Aha!" Mr. Kaplan beamed. "*Chen*nink! I tought you said '*Cha*nnink!'"

Mr. "Chennink" smiled feebly. He was a realist.

"As I was saying, Mr. Parkhill suggested that we spend the first part of the period in what he calls Open Questions. I have been told you keep notes of the questions you may wish to ask. If you will refer to them now, please, for *just* a few minutes . . . Everybody, now!"

The students seemed a little breath-taken by this gust of energetic tutelage. Then there were shrugs, exchanges of glances, and sighs of adjustment; the beginners' grade girded its scholastic loins for Open Questions. Notebooks, foolscap pages, envelopes, scraps of paper, even chewing-gum wrappers appeared, to be studied for the great event. A fat woman seemed to be reading the wall just above Mr. Jennings' head, seeking inspiration. She moaned as she waited for the light to descend. A man with a conspicuous gold tooth fumbled through his pock-

ets. Mr. Hyman Kaplan, for whom Mr. Jennings already felt a certain respect, merely leaned
his head to one side, half-closed his eyes, and whispered, "So now is Haupen Qvastions! My!" His
whispers left nothing to be desired in the way of
audibility. "Esk Titcher *abot a room goink arond.*"

"Pardon?" Mr. Jennings asked quickly. "I didn't
hear what you were saying."

Mr. Kaplan opened his eyes. "I vasn't sayink,"
he murmured dreamily. "I vas *tinking.*"

Mr. Kaplan continued "tinking." "Esk Titcher,"
he whispered. "Abot *a room goink arond!*" Mr.
Jennings felt a damp sensation on his brow. "Abot
so-an'-so! Esk Titcher . . . abot *a room goink
arond!* . . . Abot *so-an'-so!*"

For some strange reason a quotation flashed
through Mr. Jennings' mind: "That way madness
lies." Mr. Jennings fought it down.

"Esk Titcher . . . Abot—"

"Let us begin," Mr. Jennings said with calculated
briskness. "We shall recite in order, starting with—
with the lady in the back row, please."

That would leave Mr. Kaplan and his cryptic
"room goink arond," to say nothing of "so-an'-so!",
almost to the end. Mr. Jennings caught himself hop-

ing that the recess bell would ring before Mr. Kaplan's turn came. This was contrary to all that Mr. Jennings had been taught in Education V (Professor Heppelhauser's Education V) and he felt ashamed of himself.

Mr. Kaplan opened his eyes with an injured air. "*Goldboig* foist," he whispered sadly. "Oi!" His expression was that of a man betrayed.

Miss Goldberg wanted to know whether "trumpet" had anything to do with bridge, "like, with my Jeck I trumpet." After this brilliant beginning, Mr. Weinstein sought aid with the orthography of "Tsintsinnati," where his brother and "fife" children lived. (He hadn't been able to find "Tsintsinnati" in the dictionary, so he said; he admitted, however, that it was a *cheap* dictionary.) Mrs. Moskowitz asked whether "Specific" was the name of the *other* ocean. (The Atlantic and the Specific.) Miss Mitnick, obviously a superior student, was puzzled by the difference between "beside" and "besides" and, after Mr. Jennings had analyzed the distinction, between "loan," "borrow," and "lend."

Through all these weighty matters Mr. Kaplan sat with heroic resignation. Occasionally he indulged in wistful and philosophic sighs.

Miss Shirley Ziev inquired whether there wasn't something queer about the interrogative form, "When did you came, Morris?" Mr. Marcus, confessing it was probably a silly point, asked if the "state alienist" was the officer in charge of immigration and citizen papers. Miss Caravello ventured to query what the "G" in "G men" stood for.

Mr. Jennings treated each of these problems with profound earnestness. Mr. Jennings was, indeed, lost in the sweet delirium of the pedagogical chase. He was exhilarated by the challenge of communication. He was tasting, as never before in his year and a half of practice teaching, the simple joys of the schoolman. And before he knew it, with a good ten minutes to spare, it was Mr. Kaplan's turn.

"Mr. Kaplan," he said slowly, and something in him went taut.

Mr. Kaplan's face took on the luster of ecstasy. "My!" he breathed semi-publicly. "Now is commink *mine* time!" This was journey's end, Ultima Thule, the last, for which the first was made.

Mr. Kaplan rose. No other student had risen, but there was something eminently fitting, almost teleological, about Mr. Kaplan's rising. Mr. Pinsky observed every motion of the ascent with the humility of a weaker spirit. A rustle, compact of anticipation, pleasure, and anxiety, went through the classroom.

"Ladies an' gantleman," Mr. Kaplan began in his finest oratorical manner. "Mr. Pockheel told us, a lonk time beck awreddy, dat if ve vant to *loin*, den avery place ve goink, ve should vatchink for mistakes, for Haupen Qvastions. In de sopvay, on de stritt, in de alevatits—poblic or private, day an' night, alvays ve should be *stoodents!* Believe me, dat vas a fine, smot idea!" Mrs. Moskowitz nodded reverently, as if to a reading of the Psalms. "So like Mr. Pockheel said, avery place I vas goink, I vas vatchink, vatchink—" Mr. Kaplan narrowed his eyes and looked suspicious to lend authenticity to his "vatchink, vatchink"— "—all de time vatchink for tings I should esk by Haupen Qvastions time!"

This, Mr. Jennings sensed, was the introduction. It was.

"So de foist qvastion. Vat's de minnink fromm '*A room is goink arond*'?"

" 'A room is going around?' " repeated Mr. Jennings, though he knew perfectly well what Mr. Kaplan's words had been.

" 'A room is goink arond!' " Mr. Kaplan repeated firmly, and sat down.

The beginners' grade was hushed.

"Yes . . . 'A room is going around.' " There was no doubt about it: Mr. Jennings was fighting for time. "Well, the meaning of the words is perfectly simple, Mr. Kaplan. As anyone can tell—" Mr. Jennings explained the meaning of the words. He treated them individually, collectively, conceptually. But he admitted that the phrase, as a phrase, seemed strange. "Of course, if one were dizzy, or faint, or *drunk*"—Mr. Jennings was not the type to mince words—"why, then one *would* say, 'I feel as if the room is going around.' "

Mr. Norman Bloom snickered. "*I* think that's a crazy quastion!"

Mr. Kaplan surveyed Mr. Bloom with a haughty glance. "Mine dear Bloom," he said with dignity. "To *som* pipple is even de *bast* qvastions crazy!"

Mr. Bloom collapsed.

"Could you tell us exactly how you heard the phrase?" Mr. Jennings suggested quickly, fearful of the heights to which Mr. Kaplan's scorn might ascend.

Mr. Kaplan nodded. "Fromm mine vife. She vas talkink to Mrs. Skolsky—dat's de lady livink op-stairs—abot Mrs. Backer—dat's de femily livink *don*stairs. An' Mrs. Skolsky said, 'You know, I tink Mrs. Backer vill saparate Mr. Backer mit divorce!' So mine vife esked, netcheral, 'So how you know?' So Mrs. Skolsky gave enswer: 'Averybody's sayink dat! *A room is goink arond!'* "

" 'A *rumor's* going around!' " cried Mr. Jennings. Meaning burst within him, like a fire-cracker. "A *'rumor'* is going around, Mr. Kaplan! Why, that's an *excellent* phrase! A 'rumor' refers to—"

But Mr. Kaplan hardly listened. His smile was phosphorescent. He dropped rays of sweet redemption over his shoulders, right and left. For Mr. Norman Bloom, staring moodily at the floor, Mr. Kaplan had a special and triumphant radiance.

When Mr. Jennings had given his all to "A rumor's going around," Mr. Kaplan murmured, "My! Dat vas som qvastion!" (There was a fine objectivity in the awe with which Mr. Kaplan regarded his brain-children.) Then he asked his second question.

"I hoid soch an axpression, I can't believe. Also, it sonds fonny. *Fonny,*" Mr. Kaplan repeated with a telling glance at Mr. Norman Bloom, "not crazy. Plizz, vat's de minnink fromm 'so-an'-so,' a 'so-an'-so'?"

It had come.

"Do you want me to explain 'so-and-so,' or '*a* so-and-so'? There is a distinction, you know." Mr. Jennings faced the worst bravely.

"Awright, lat be '*a* so-an'-so,'" said Mr. Kaplan, with a benign wave of the hand.

Mr. Jennings took a deep breath. Education V, and the pedantic wisdom of Professor Heppelhauser, seemed to be so far away, so abstract, so totally worthless in dealing with problems of the magnitude of "a so-and-so."

"The phrase 'a so-and-so,'" he began earnestly, "is heard quite commonly. But it's vulgar. It's used, really, instead of—well, profanity."

Mr. Jennings paused hopefully, ready to go no further. But in the eyes of the class there was no flicker of understanding to the concept "profanity." Mr. Jennings faced the task of explaining profanity without using it.

"Profanity means—well, cursing, swearing, using bad, foul, *not nice* language." Still the faces were in blank repose; still the eyes held no flame of recognition. "Let me put it this way, class. Suppose John, say, wants to—"

"Who is dat 'John'?" asked Mr. Kaplan promptly.

Mr. Jennings' hands felt scaly. "Any John, Mr. Kaplan. I use the name only as a sample."

"My!" Mr. Kaplan exclaimed, admiring Mr. Jennings' ingenuity.

"Suppose *someone*, then, wants to say something bad about someone else, wants to *curse* him, really—but doesn't actually want to use profane language. Well, he'll say, 'He's a so-and-so!' instead of—" Too late did young Mr. Jennings realize that he had gone too far. "Instead of—" The class waited expectantly, Miss Mitnick with a blush, *crescendo*. "Instead of—"

"Low-life! Tremp! Goot-fa-nottink!" cried Mr. Kaplan impetuously.

"Yes! Fine! Exactly!" Never had Mr. Jennings been so grateful. "That's *precisely* how 'a so-and-so' is used!"

An "Ah!" of illumination went through the class. But Mr. Bloom glowered. "That's a bad quastion to ask with ladies in room!" he cried out.

Two hot camps of thought sprang up. The room buzzed with argument, defense, recrimination. Mrs. Moskowitz supported Mr. Bloom indignantly. Mr. Marcus, aided by many a sarcastic gibe from Mr.

Pinsky, rallied to the Kaplan banner. Mr. Jennings looked bewildered.

"Aha!" Mr. Kaplan's war cry resounded against the walls. "Who is sayink mine qvastion is bed? Who? *In aducation is no bed qvastions!*"

And the opposition fell into shamed silence. On Mr. Kaplan's face there shone a glow which, without a doubt, meant *"Honi soit qui mal y pense."* "De kind 'so-an'-so' *I* minn, Mr. Chennink," Mr. Kaplan said in a clarion voice, *"isn't* volgar, or de odder ting!"

"Profane," Mr. Jennings ventured.

"Or 'profane,' like you say. I minn altogadder difference, plizz."

Mr. Jennings took counsel with his soul. He had done his duty with patience and discretion. And yet, undaunted, Mr. Kaplan pursued some strange, evasive Truth. It was in a voice freighted with caution that Mr. Jennings said, "Perhaps you had better illustrate what you mean, Mr. Kaplan."

Mr. Kaplan rose for the last time that memorable night. The raindrops did impish gavottes on the panes, and the room echoed their derision.

"Vell, lest veek I mat in de stritt mine old frand Moe Slavitt," Mr. Kaplan began, *sotto voce.*

" 'Hollo, Moe!' I said. 'How you fillink dis beauriful mornink?' So Moe said, 'I got in mine had a hadake.' So I esk, 'Noo, a *bed* hadake, Moe?' So he gives enswer, 'Not a tarrible hadake, but also not *not* a hadake.' Dat Moe—alvays he's sayink Yas an' No mit de same brat! So I said, 'Leesen, Moe! Don' talkink all de time in reedles! I esk a tsimple qvastion, so give, plizz, a strong, plain enswer. Do—you—fill—Hau—Kay: *Yas or No?*' Vell, vat Moe did? Ha! He made like dis mit his shouldiss—" Mr. Kaplan shrugged his "shouldiss" with profound expressiveness—"an' said, 'I don' fill rotten, I don' fill A. Number Vun. *I'm just so-an'-so!*' "

The recess bell rang. And the raindrops, conscious of their destiny, howled on the steamy windows, like madmen.

K*A*P*L*A*N
AND PYTHIAS

NO trumpets blared as the fat little man entered the classroom. He was roly-poly and ruddy. He had a tiny nose and a reddish mustache. His mustache was so thick that it made his nose seem incredibly small. He looked like a fat little Buddha—a Buddha with a mustache. He walked up to Mr. Parkhill's desk and, without a word, handed him a card. It read:

VISITOR'S CARD

AMERICAN NIGHT PREPARATORY SCHOOL

FOR ADULTS

PLEASE ADMIT THE BEARER: *Mr. Teitelman*

FOR ONE TRIAL LESSON.

Leland Robinson

Principal

M. S.

The names had been written in in the clear hand of Miss Schnepfe, Mr. Robinson's secretary. (Miss

Schnepfe's first name was Leona, but she had fallen
into the strange habit of signing her initials as
"M. S." Sometimes, clinging to her sex, she used
"Miss S.")

"Mr.—er—Teitelman?" asked Mr. Parkhill.

The fat little man nodd'd. He seemed very sad.

"Just take a seat, please, anywhere." Mr. Parkhill
smiled reassuringly. He was careful to treat new students and visitors with particular kindliness; he
knew how choked with embarrassment most of them
were. "And please consider yourself a member of
the class for the evening. I hope you will—er—enter
into the work just as if you were one of our regular
students. I hope you *will* be after tonight."

The fat little man looked at the rows of chairs,
then walked to an empty place in the front row without a word. He sat down. Mrs. Tomasic was on his
left. Mr. Hyman Kaplan was on his right.

"Valcome!" said Mr. Kaplan to the newcomer
with a fine generosity.

The fat little man seemed startled.

Mr. Parkhill smiled encouragingly at the visitor
and said: "We shall devote the first half of the class
session tonight to finishing the Recitation and Speech
exercise of last Thursday. As I recall, we have still

to hear from—let me see—Mrs. Moskowitz, Mr.
Pinsky, Miss Kowalski, and—er—yes, Mr. Marcus."
The four students named stirred uneasily. "Suppose
we allow these students a few minutes to prepare
themselves. . . . The rest of the class can study the
list of spelling words on page ninety-six of 'English
for Beginners.' "

The class began to rustle through "English for
Beginners." The four fated to recite went through
individual rites of preparation. Mr. Pinsky, a sea-
soned orator, muttered and made motions with his
hand. Miss Kowalski knit her brows and tried to
memorize something from her notebook. Mr. Marcus
looked sour. As for Mrs. Moskowitz—she heaved
low moans of despair and prayed to some unknown
deity.

Mr. Hyman Kaplan paid no attention to these
matters. He was examining the fat little man on his
left, curiously, insistently, out of the corner of his
left eye. Mr. Kaplan had an independent nervous
system for each orb: his left eye scrutinized the fat
little man; his right, like a sentry, was trained on
Mr. Parkhill. It was uncanny.

For a long moment Mr. Kaplan subjected the visitor to his most critical gaze, his left eye glittering

like a bright lens. It was clear to Mr. Parkhill that Mr. Kaplan, to whom every mortal was a direct personal challenge, was trying to discover whether this newcomer was friend or foe. When the examination had been pursued to Mr. Kaplan's satisfaction, he leaned his head to the left and whispered, in a tone just loud enough to be heard by everyone in the room, "How's by you de name, plizz?"

The fat little man looked sadly at Mr. Kaplan and said nothing.

Mr. Kaplan cleared his throat. "Eh . . . How—is—by—you—de—*name*—plizz?" His whisper was more compelling.

The fat little man took a fountain pen out of his pocket and, without turning his head, laid it on the arm of his chair. A name was stamped in black on the barrel of the pen.

" 'F. Teitelman,' " Mr. Kaplan read, his eyes gleaming. "Aha! 'F'—for Philip, ha?"

The fat little man shook his head.

"*Not* for Philip?" Amazement was in Mr. Kaplan's voice. "My!" He closed his eyes, pursed his lips, and pondered on this baffling matter. Then he whispered politely: "So vat *is* by you de name, vill you be so kindly?"

"Jerome," said the fat little man.

Mr. Kaplan covered his eyes with one hand and murmured, "Jerome. . . . *Jerome*. . . . Dat's mit a 'G'!" Mr. Kaplan's eyes opened wide. "So vy is on de fontain pan—"

Suspicion stared out of Mr. Kaplan's eyes like a placard.

" 'Jerome' you sayink, ha?" he whispered tensely. "*So vy is on de pan 'F'?*" There was a ring of accusation in his voice. Mr. Kaplan watched every move the fat little man made. He devoted particular attention to the mustache.

The fat little man looked at Mr. Kaplan more sadly than ever, and said: "De pan belongs mine vife."

"I think we are ready to start now," Mr. Parkhill announced. He had been fascinated by the little drama in the front row. "Er—Mrs. Moskowitz, will you speak first, please?"

Mrs. Moskowitz sighed "I s'pose," rose, smoothed her dress, stumbled over Mr. Scymzak's feet, apologized with a quick "Axcusing!", ran her hand across her hair, coughed, almost dropped her purse, and smiled a weak greeting to Miss Mitnick—all in the time it took her to walk from her seat in the second row to the front of the room.

"Sobject—'About Arond De House.'"

Mr. Kaplan shot the fat little man a "You-see-what-I-have-to-go-through!" look. Mrs. Moskowitz generally spoke of those aspects of life which dealt with something "arond de house." Mrs. Moskowitz did not lead a very rich existence.

"De men don't know how hard is de life for de ladies," she said. "De men tink—"

"'*Men* don't know how hard *life* is for *women*'—not 'ladies,'" Mr. Parkhill interrupted. "You mean men and women in general, Mrs. Moskowitz. You remember our exercise on definite and indefinite articles, don't you?"

Mrs. Moskowitz tried to produce an expression of comprehension.

"Soch a fine titcher ve got," Mr. Kaplan whispered to the fat little man, smiling. The face of Buddha was immobile. Mr. Kaplan sighed; he was making no headway on the fraternal road.

Mrs. Moskowitz began all over again. "*Men* don't know how hard is *life* of *women*. Som of the—no—som women work in shop all day, I do, and by night must comming home, clinn op de house, making sopper, take care of children if have children, which I have, fix clothes, and so far."

Mrs. Moskowitz stopped, exhausted. She had over-taxed her imagination in that one great flight. "So vat more I should tell?"

"Abot feexing claws!" Mr. Kaplan cried out. "Tell abot feexing claws!" He gazed proudly at the fat little man to see whether *this* maneuver would win any response. The fat little man blew his nose. In sheer desperation Mr. Kaplan whispered: "Teitelman, don' be afraid! You should givink ideas too!"

The fat little man looked at Mr. Kaplan for a moment, expressionless. Then, and it was all the more impressive because it was so unexpected, he nodded his head vigorously three times. The warm, triumphant smile flooded Mr. Kaplan's countenance. Teitelman *was* his friend. *Semper fidelis.*

"Awright, so like Mr. Kaplan says," Mrs. Moskowitz announced. "About fixing clothes I'll tell. Vell, for fixing clothes or shoits or socks, you should have a niddle, a spool trad de same color, and also a little —eh—how you say—"

"Time!" said the fat little man suddenly.

The students turned their heads in surprise. Visitors never recited. Here was a man of a new order.

Mr. Kaplan, grinning with enormous delight, cried, "*Fine*, Teitelman! Dat's de boy!"

Mrs. Moskowitz stared at the fat little man, dazed. Then she blinked her eyes indignantly. "Vy about *time* all of a sodden? For fixing clothes you should have niddle, trad—but vat's got to do *time?*"

"You nid time *too*, netcheral," Mr. Kaplan suggested promptly, with a nod to his new bosom friend.

Mrs. Moskowitz turned on Mr. Kaplan with scorn. "And you should have a chair also, for sitting, and laktric lights you should see, and a house for being insite. So do I have to tell *all* about if I'm talking about sewing somting?"

Mr. Parkhill interceded hastily. "I'm sure our visitor didn't mean any harm, Mrs. Moskowitz. He didn't—er—quite understand. Do go on."

Mrs. Moskowitz gave Messrs. Kaplan and Teitelman a smirk, aware that she had gained a telling prestige-point. Mr. Kaplan whispered consolation to the fat little man. "Tsall right, Teitelman. It's Hau Kay! *Give ideas!*"

Mrs. Moskowitz continued with great dignity. "So like I said, you should have a niddle, trad, and somting alse. Maybe you having a tick piece goods, like mine Oscar's overcoat, and you ken't pushing trough de niddle, so you put on de finger a little kind cop, fromm tin it's made ot. It's called a—"

"Dumb-bell!" said the fat little man.

The class gasped. Miss Mitnick blushed for Mrs. Moskowitz. Mr. Bloom shook his head. Mr. Kaplan squirmed in his seat with delight at this, the coming of age of his ward. Mrs. Moskowitz pressed her lips together and then in one long, uninterrupted breath blurted out: "Mister-I-dunno-*who*-you-are—"

"De name is Teitelman," said Mr. Kaplan proudly.

"—*I* don't mean dumb-bell! Maybe *your* vife is using dumb-bells. I use a *timble!*" Wrapped in her wrath, Mrs. Moskowitz was like a Valkyrie, spear and all. "Now I'll go farder. So if you have niddle, trad, and *timble*, please, de rast is easy." She paused. "You fill op de holes."

Mrs. Moskowitz stopped. She was perspiring. (Mrs. Moskowitz paid a heavy toll whenever she wrestled with ideas.) Her eyes clouded now, as she sought inspiration to go on. "I s'pose I should talk som more," she muttered miserably. The class waited for Mrs. Moskowitz to "talk som more." The silence was painful. Suddenly, like a thunderbolt,

inspiration came. "Also arond de house is to *cook!*"
New vistas opened before Mrs. Moskowitz. "Cooking is to me like painting maybe to artist. I love.
Since I'm ten yiss old I'm cooking. I bake brat—rye
and pumpernickel—rolls, cookeess, even—"

"Pies!" cried the fat little man.

"CAKE!" retorted Mrs. Moskowitz hotly. "*Not*
pies, Mister. Cake! K-A-K-E!"

Like a falcon Mr. Kaplan swooped to the defense
of his protégé. "You makink pies *too,* no?"

"I—bake—CAKE!"

"Moskovitz, don' gat axcited!" Mr. Kaplan exclaimed. "Mine frand Teitelman is tryink to *halpink*
you. He's tryink to say you an A Number Vun cook.
You *got* to bakink pies!"

"Batter Mister New Student should halping
you!" shouted Mrs. Moskowitz with fury. "Me he's
telling dumb-bells for timbles, time all of a sodden,
and now he's even trowing in *pies!* Dat's enoff!"

She stalked to her seat, her head high. The classroom roared with excitement. In this dazzling, hectic
interchange there was the seed of a great feud. Miss
Goldberg sent waves of sympathy to Mrs. Moskowitz. Miss Mitnick, fear in her eyes, was pale. Mr.
Norman Bloom kept going "Tchk! Tchk! Always
troubles!"

Mr. Parkhill, overcome by embarrassment, tried to placate Mrs. Moskowitz. He apologized for the new student's excessive eagerness. He assured Mrs. Moskowitz that no one had meant to offend her. He urged her to continue. It was of no avail. Where *l'honneur* was concerned, Sadie Moskowitz was not the type to be bought with light phrases. She shook her head stubbornly. The class buzzed with the scandal.

And Messrs. Kaplan and Teitelman sat in the front row oblivious of the tempest which seethed around them. They seemed united by a mighty bond. They looked like men who had faced death together. They paid no attention to the speech of Mr. Pinsky which followed. They offered no objection to the linguistic mutilations of Miss Kowalski. They let pass, without so much as a murmur, the various phonetic extravagances of Simon Marcus. They just sat, these two, like men caught in the surge of a common memory.

The recess bell rang. The classroom filled with happy noises. Mr. Kaplan smiled at the fat little man and said, "Lat's goink otside now." The fat little man shook his head sadly. Mr. Kaplan said, "Hau Kay, Teitelman. You *rast*. Tink op som more fine ideas." He went into the corridor, beaming.

The fat little man sat in the room, staring at Mr. Parkhill. There were just the two of them now. The fat little man seemed to be thinking. After a few moments he took his hat, said "Goombye," and left.

When Mr. Kaplan returned, after the recess, he found his comrade in arms gone. "Who seen Teitelman?" he cried, in pain.

No one had seen Teitelman. No one seemed to know what had happened to the fat little man. Mr. Parkhill called on Miss Caravello and the reading exercise began.

But Mr. Kaplan sat plunged in a moody silence. For the rest of the night gloom enveloped him, like a shroud. He did not participate in the reading drill. He did not call out daring thoughts for vocabulary exercise. The heart seemed to have gone out of Hyman Kaplan. Lost was the great flair.

Only once did Mr. Kaplan emerge from the abyss. That was when, staring wistfully at the empty seat beside him, on which the fat little man had left his "Visitor's Card" as an eloquent souvenir, Mr. Kaplan sighed the sigh of the heavy-laden and murmured: "My! I lost a *fine* frand."

MR. K*A*P*L*A*N
AND SHAKESPEARE

IT was Miss Higby's idea in the first place. She had suggested to Mr. Parkhill that the students came to her class unaware of the *finer* side of English, of its beauty and, as she put it, "the glorious heritage of our literature." She suggested that perhaps poetry might be worked into the exercises of Mr. Parkhill's class. The beginners' grade had, after all, been subjected to almost a year of English and might be presumed to have achieved some linguistic sophistication. Poetry would make the students conscious of precise enunciation; it would make them read with greater care and an ear for sounds. Miss Higby, who had once begun a master's thesis on Coventry Patmore, *loved* poetry. And, it should be said in all justice, she argued her cause with considerable logic. Poetry *would* be excellent for the enunciation of the students, thought Mr. Parkhill.

So it was that when he faced the class the following Tuesday night, Mr. Parkhill had a volume of

Shakespeare on his desk, and an eager, almost an expectant, look in his eye. The love that Miss Higby bore for poetry in general was as nothing compared to the love that Mr. Parkhill bore for Shakespeare in particular. To Mr. Parkhill, poetry meant Shakespeare. Many years ago he had played Polonius in his senior class play.

"Tonight, class," said Mr. Parkhill, "I am going to try an experiment."

The class looked up dutifully. They had come to regard Mr. Parkhill's pedagogical innovations as part of the natural order.

"I am going to introduce you to poetry—great poetry. You see—" Mr. Parkhill delivered a modest lecture on the beauty of poetry, its expression of the loftier thoughts of men, its economy of statement. He hoped it would be a relief from spelling and composition exercises to use poetry as the subject matter of the regular Recitation and Speech period. "I shall write a passage on the board and read it for you. Then, for Recitation and Speech, you will give short addresses, using the passage as the general topic, telling us what it has brought to your minds, what thoughts and ideas."

The class seemed quite pleased by the announce-
ment. Miss Mitnick blushed happily. (This blush
was different from most of Miss Mitnick's blushes;
there was aspiration and idealism in it.) Mr. Norman
Bloom sighed with a business-like air: you could tell
that for him poetry was merely another assignment,
like a speech on "What I Like to Eat Best" or a composition on "A Day at a Picnic." Mrs. Moskowitz,
to whom any public performance was unpleasant,
tried to look enthusiastic, without much success. And
Mr. Hyman Kaplan, the heroic smile on his face as
indelibly as ever, looked at Mr. Parkhill with admiration and whispered to himself: "Poyetry! Now
is poyetry! My! Mus' be progriss ve makink awreddy!"

"The passage will be from Shakespeare," Mr.
Parkhill announced, opening the volume.

An excited buzz ran through the class as the magic
of that name fell upon them.

"Imachine!" murmured Mr. Kaplan. "Jakesbeer!"

"*Shake*speare, Mr. Kaplan!"

Mr. Parkhill took a piece of chalk and, with care
and evident love, wrote the following passage on the
board in large, clear letters:

Tomorrow, and tomorrow, and tomorrow
Creeps in this petty pace from day to day,
To the last syllable of recorded time;
And all our yesterdays have lighted fools
The way to dusty death. Out, out, brief candle!
Life's but a walking shadow, a poor player
That struts and frets his hour upon the stage,
And then is heard no more; it is a tale
Told by an idiot, full of sound and fury,
Signifying nothing.

A reverent hush filled the classroom, as eyes gazed with wonder on this passage from the Bard. Mr. Parkhill was pleased at this.

"I shall read the passage first," he said. "Listen carefully to my enunciation—and—er—let Shake, speare's thoughts sink into your minds."

Mr. Parkhill read: " 'Tomorrow, and tomorrow, and tomorrow . . .' " Mr. Parkhill read very well and this night, as if some special fire burned in him, he read with rare eloquence. "Out, out, brief candle!" In Miss Mitnick's eyes there was inspiration and wonder. "Life's but a walking shadow . . ." Mrs. Moskowitz sat with a heavy frown, indicating cerebration. "It is a tale told by an idiot . . ." Mr. Kaplan's smile had taken on something luminous;

but his eyes were closed: it was not clear whether Mr. Kaplan had surrendered to the spell of the Immortal Bard or to that of Morpheus.

"I shall—er—read the passage again," said Mr. Parkhill, clearing his throat vociferously until he saw Mr. Kaplan's eyes open. " 'Tomorrow, and tomorrow, and tomorrow. . . .' "

When Mr. Parkhill had read the passage for the second time, he said: "That should be quite clear now. Are there any questions?"

There were a few questions. Mr. Scymzak wanted to know whether "frets" was "a little kind excitement." Miss Schneiderman asked about "struts." Mr. Kaplan wasn't sure about "cripps." Mr. Parkhill explained the words carefully, with several illustrative uses of each word. "No more questions? Well, I shall allow a few minutes for you all to—er —think over the meaning of the passage. Then we shall begin Recitation and Speech."

Mr. Kaplan promptly closed his eyes again, his smile beatific. The students sank into that revery miscalled thought, searching their souls for the symbols evoked by Shakespeare's immortal words.

"Miss Caravello, will you begin?" asked Mr. Parkhill at last.

Miss Caravello went to the front of the room. "Da poem isa gooda," she said slowly. "Itsa have—"

"It *has*."

"It hasa beautiful wordsa. Itsa lak Dante, Italian poet—"

"Ha!" cried Mr. Kaplan scornfully. "Shaksbeer you metchink mit Tante? *Shaksbeer?* Mein Gott!"

It was obvious that Mr. Kaplan had identified himself with Shakespeare and would tolerate no disparagement of his *alter ego*.

"Miss Caravello is merely expressing her own ideas," said Mr. Parkhill pacifically. (Actually, he felt completely sympathetic to Mr. Kaplan's point of view.)

"Hau Kay," agreed Mr. Kaplan, with a generous wave of the hand. "But to me is no comparink a high-cless man like Shaksbeer mit a Tante, dat's all."

Miss Caravello, her poise shattered, said a few more words and sat down.

Mrs. Yampolsky's contribution was brief. "This is full deep meanings," she said, her eyes on the floor. "Is hard for a person not so good in English to unnistand. But I like."

" '*Like!*' " cried Mr. Kaplan with a fine impatience.

" *'Like?'* Batter *love*, Yampolsky. Mit Shaksbeer mus' be *love!*"

Mr. Parkhill had to suggest that Mr. Kaplan control his aesthetic passions. He did understand how Mr. Kaplan felt, however, and sensed a new bond between them. Mrs. Yampolsky staggered through several more nervous comments and retired.

Mr. Bloom was next. He gave a long declamation, ending: "So is passimistic ideas in the poem, and I am optimist. Life should be happy—so we should remember this is only a poem. Maybe is Shakespeare too passimistic."

"You wronk, Bloom!" cried Mr. Kaplan with prompt indignation. "Shaksbeer is passimist because is de *life* passimist also!"

Mr. Parkhill, impressed by this philosophical stroke, realized that Mr. Kaplan, afire with the glory of the Swan of Avon, could not be suppressed. Mr. Kaplan was the kind of man who brooked no criticism of his gods. The only solution was to call on Mr. Kaplan for his recitation at once. Mr. Parkhill was, indeed, curious about what fresh thoughts Mr. Kaplan would utter after his passionate defences of the Bard. When Mr. Parkhill had corrected certain parts of Mr. Bloom's speech, emphasizing Mr. Bloom's failure to use the indefinite article, he said: "Mr. Kaplan, will *you* speak next?"

Mr. Kaplan's face broke into a glow; his smile was like a rainbow. "Soitinly," he said, walking to the front of the room. Never had he seemed so dignified, so eager, so conscious of a great destiny.

"Er—Mr. Kaplan," added Mr. Parkhill, suddenly aware of the possibilities which the situation (Kaplan on Shakespeare) involved: "Speak *carefully*."

"*Spacially* careful vill I be," Mr. Kaplan reassured him. He cleared his throat, adjusted his tie, and began: "Ladies an' gantleman, you hoid all kinds minninks abot dis piece poyetry, an'—"

"*Poetry*."

"—abot dis piece *po*etry. But to me is a difference minnink altogadder. Ve mus' tink abot Julius Scissor an' how *he* falt!"

Mr. Parkhill moved nervously, puzzled.

"In dese exact voids is Julius Scissor sayink—"

"Er—Mr. Kaplan," said Mr. Parkhill once he grasped the full import of Mr. Kaplan's error. "The passage is from 'Macbeth.' "

Mr. Kaplan looked at Mr. Parkhill with injured surprise. "*Not* fromm 'Julius Scissor'?" There was pain in his voice.

"No. And it's—er—'Julius *Cae*sar.' "

Mr. Kaplan waited until the last echo of the name had permeated his soul. "Podden me, Mr. Pockheel. Isn't '*see*zor' vat you cottink somting op mit?"

"That," said Mr. Parkhill quickly, "is 'scissor.' You have used 'Caesar' for 'scissor' and 'scissor' for 'Caesar.' "

Mr. Kaplan nodded, marvelling at his own virtuosity.

"But go on with your speech, please." Mr. Parkhill, to tell the truth, felt a little guilty that he had not announced at the very beginning that the passage was from "Macbeth." "Tell us *why* you thought the lines were from 'Julius Caesar.' "

"Vell," said Mr. Kaplan to the class, his smile assuming its normal serenity. "I vas positif, becawss I can *see* de whole ting." He paused, debating how to explain this cryptic remark. Then his eyes filled with a strange enchantment. "I see de whole scinn. It's in a tant, on de night bafore dey makink Julius de Kink fromm Rome. So he is axcited an' ken't slip.

He is layink in bad, tinking: 'Tomorrow an' tomorrow an' tomorrow. How slow dey movink! Almost cripps! Soch a pity de pace!' "

Before Mr. Parkhill could explain that "petty pace" did not mean "Soch a pity de pace!" Mr. Kaplan had soared on.

"De days go slow, fromm day to day, like leetle tsyllables on phonograph racords fromm time."

Anxiety and bewilderment invaded Mr. Parkhill's eyes.

" 'An' vat abot yestidday?' tinks Julius Scissor. Ha! 'All our yestiddays are only makink a good light for fools to die in de dost!' "

" 'Dusty death' doesn't mean—" There was no interrupting Mr. Kaplan.

"An' Julius Scissor is so tired, an' he vants to fallink aslip. So he hollers, mit fillink, 'Go ot! Go ot! Short candle!' So it goes ot."

Mr. Kaplan's voice dropped to a whisper. "But he ken't slip. Now is bodderink him de idea fromm life. 'Vat is de life altogadder?' tinks Julius Scissor. An' he gives enswer, de pot I like de bast. 'Life is like a bum actor, strottink an' hollerink arond de stage for only vun hour bafore he's kicked ot. Life is a tale told by idjots, dat's all, full of fonny sonds an' phooey!' "

Mr. Parkhill could be silent no longer. " 'Full of sound and fury!' " he cried desperately. But inspiration, like an irresistible force, swept Mr. Kaplan on.

" 'Life is monkey business! It don' minn a ting. It signifies nottink!' An' den Julius Scissor closes his ice fest—" Mr. Kaplan demonstrated the Consul's exact ocular process in closing his "ice"—"—an' falls dad!"

The class was hushed as Mr. Kaplan stopped. In the silence, a tribute to the fertility of Mr. Kaplan's imagination and the power of his oratory, Mr. Kaplan went to his seat. But just before he sat down, as if adding a postscript, he sighed: "Dat vas mine idea. But ufcawss is all wronk, becawss Mr. Pockheel said de voids ain't abot Julius Scissor altogadder. It's all abot an Irishman by de name Macbat."

Then Mr. Kaplan sat down.

It was some time before Mr. Parkhill could bring himself to criticize Mr. Kaplan's pronunciation, enunciation, diction, grammar, idiom, and sentence structure. For Mr. Parkhill discovered that he could not easily return to the world of reality. He was still trying to tear himself away from that tent outside

Rome, where "Julius Scissor," cursed with insomnia, had thought of time and life—and philosophized himself to a strange and sudden death.

Mr. Parkhill was distinctly annoyed with Miss Higby.

THE TERRIBLE
VENGEANCE OF
H*Y*M*A*N K*A*P*L*A*N

MR. PARKHILL wondered whether he had not been a little rash in taking up Idioms with the beginners' grade. Idioms were, of course, of primary importance to those who sought an understanding of English: they were of the very essence of the language. At the last session of the class, Mr. Parkhill had spent a careful hour in explaining what idioms were, how they grew, how they took on meaning. He had illustrated his lecture with many examples, drawn from "English for Beginners." He had answered questions. And for homework, he had assigned what seemed a simple enough exercise: three short sentences, using an idiom in each sentence. But now Mr. Parkhill realized that he had been too optimistic. The assignment was not proving a success. It was, in truth, incredible.

Mr. Marcus, for example, had used the expression: "It will cost you free." That, to Mr. Marcus, was an idiom. Mrs. Tomasic had submitted only one sentence, as much as confessing that her imagination quailed before the magnitude of the assignment. The sentence was "Honestly is the best policy." Mr. Jacob Rubin was groping in the right direction, at least; he seemed to suspect what an idiom *was;* and yet, for one of his efforts, he had given: "By twelve a.m. the job will be as good as down."

And now, a full half-hour before the end of the period, it was time for the contribution of Mr. Hyman Kaplan. There they were, on the board: three sentences—under a heading which was like an illuminated marquee:

3 SENT. (& ID.)

by

H * Y * M * A * N   K * A * P * L * A * N

(Mr. Parkhill had learned that trying to dissuade Mr. Kaplan from printing his name in all its starry splendor, on the slightest provocation, was just a waste of time.)

"Mr. Kaplan, read your sentences, please," said Mr. Parkhill briskly.

The briskness was quite intentional; it buttressed Mr. Parkhill's morale. The class had snickered sev-

eral times while reading the sentences which Mr.
Kaplan had written on the blackboard; now, with
Mr. Kaplan to read them, there was no telling to
what heights their emotions might ascend.

Mr. Kaplan rose, his smile that of an angel in
flight. "Ladies an' gantleman an' Mr. Pockheel.
Tree santences I vas wridink on de board, mit id-
yoms. An' mine idea vas dat—"

"Please *read* the sentences," Mr. Parkhill broke
in. Mr. Kaplan was congenitally incapable of resist-
ing the urge to orate.

"I back you podden. De foist santence . . ." Mr.
Kaplan read it. He read it distinctly, and with pride.

1. He's nots.

Mr. Parkhill took a long, deep breath. "That's
not an idiom, Mr. Kaplan. That's—er—*slang*. No
one who uses English correctly, with taste, would
ever use an expression like 'He's—er—nuts.' "

Dismay crept into Mr. Kaplan's face and wrestled
with the great smile. "Is *not* a good axprassion, 'He's
nots'?" he asked, with a certain hurt. It was apparent
that Mr. Kaplan had put his heart and soul into
"He's nots."

"No, Mr. Kaplan. It's *very* bad."

Mrs. Moskowitz, large, serene, behemothian, shot Mr. Kaplan a pitying glance. "He's nots!" she crowed. It wasn't clear whether Mrs. Moskowitz was merely repeating Mr. Kaplan's words or was indulging in a little commentary of her own.

"But so many pipple are usink dese voids," Mr. Kaplan protested, shooting Mrs. Moskowitz an injured look. "Honist, avery place I'm goink I hear, 'He's nots!'"

Mr. Parkhill shook his head, adamant in the face of the *vox populi.* "It doesn't matter how many people say it, Mr. Kaplan. It's an incorrect phrase. It has no place in good English. Besides, you spelled the word—er—'nuts' wrong. It's 'n-*u*-t-s.'"

Mr. Parkhill printed "N-U-T-S" on the board. He explained what "nut" really meant, distinguishing it from "not" with care. With much feeling, he drove home the point that "He's nuts" was outlawed by the canons of good usage. And Mr. Kaplan bowed to the hegemony of the purists. He seemed a little saddened. Something in Mr. Kaplan died with the death of "He's nots."

"Mine sacond santence." The second sentence was, if anything, more astonishing than the first.

2. Get the pearls. By hook or cook!

" 'By hook or cook,' " Mr. Parkhill repeated, very softly. " 'By hook or cook' . . . Mr. Kaplan, I'm afraid you've made another serious mistake."

This was too much for Mr. Kaplan to believe. "*Also* tarrible?" he asked, his voice charged with pain. "I tought dis vould be a real high-cless idyom."

Mr. Parkhill shook his head. "You seem to have an idea of what an idiom is, in this sentence." (Mr. Kaplan shot Mrs. Moskowitz a triumphant smile.) "But you've ruined the idea by your spelling." (Mr. Kaplan's smile scurried into limbo.) "You have confused two entirely different words. What's wrong with Mr. Kaplan's sentence—anyone?"

The beginners' grade glared at Mr. Kaplan's non-Spencerian hand.

Mr. Sam Pinsky answered first. "Should be 'by hook *and* cook!' "

"No!" Mr. Parkhill exclaimed severely. "That would only make it worse."

"I think it should better be, 'By hook or *crook*,' " suggested Miss Mitnick.

"Exactly! '*Crook*,' not 'cook,' Mr. Kaplan."

Miss Mitnick lowered her eyes and smiled modestly. This had a depressing effect on Mr. Kaplan.

"I tought dat 'crook' is like a boiglar, a robber, a chitter," he objected.

"It does mean that," said Mr. Parkhill. "But the phrase 'by hook or by crook' is something altogether different. It refers to—"

Mr. Kaplan was wrapped in gloom. To be both scorned by Mrs. Moskowitz, whom he regarded with condescension, and bested by Miss Mitnick—these were blows which a man of Mr. Kaplan's mettle did not take lightly. Mr. Kaplan sighed (it was the sigh of those who have seen justice fail), and searched for his gods.

"Your third sentence, please."

Mr. Kaplan seemed a little shorter, a little more rotund, a little less bland and euphoric than usual. The disaster of his sentences had left its mark on Mr. Kaplan.

"I s'pose," he said wistfully, "dat mine toid santence vill be awful also."

It was a touching admission. Mr. Parkhill felt sorry for Mr. Kaplan. He felt worse when Mr. Kaplan read the third sentence.

3. Hang yourself in reseption hall, please.

There was a burst of laughter from Mr. Bloom, followed by peals of hilarity from Messrs. Rabinowitz and Weinstein, and reinforced by an unmaidenly guffaw from Mrs. Moskowitz. Miss Mitnick, a creature of more delicate habits, smiled shyly. Miss Kowalski placed her hands over her eyes and shook.

" 'Heng—your-salf—in—re-sap-tion—hall—plizz!' " Mr. Kaplan repeated stubbornly, clinging to the words with the love of a father for his own flesh and blood.

Mr. Parkhill waited for order to filter back into the noisy classroom. "Mr. Kaplan, you have made a rather amusing error." He said it as gently as he could. "If you will merely read the sentence carefully, and pay attention to the word-order—especially to the object of 'hang'—I'm sure you will see why the sentence struck the class as being—er—funny."

Mr. Kaplan nodded dutifully and read the sentence again, aloud. " 'Heng—your-salf—in—re-sap-tion—hall—plizz!' " He pursed his lips, wrinkled his brow, closed one eye wisely, and stared at the ceiling. This exhibition of concentration completed to his satisfaction, he whispered the sentence to himself, all over again. Everyone waited.

"Aha!" It was Mr. Kaplan's first "Aha!" of the evening, and it rang with his old courage. "I got him!" This was more like the real Hyman Kaplan, valiant, audacious. "Ufcawss! Should be *kepital ladders* on 'resaption hall'! Tsimple!"

The Mitnick-Bloom-Moskowitz *entente* was swept to new peaks of rapture. This was a rare opportunity: at last Mr. Kaplan seemed to have lost his magic talent for emerging triumphant from any predicament, however ominous. Someone cried, "*Goombye*, Mr. Keplen!" A voice said, "Oi! I'll die!"—and Mrs. Moskowitz retorted: "Yas! By henging!"

Mr. Kaplan smiled bravely: it was heart-rending. Mr. Parkhill rapped on the desk with a pointer.

"No, Mr. Kaplan," he said kindly. " 'Reception hall' is not a proper noun, so it doesn't require capital letters. 'Reception,' by the way, is spelled 'r-e-*c*-e.' No, it's the meaning of your sentence that's at fault. 'Hang *yourself* in the reception hall,' Mr. Kaplan? You don't say *that* to your guests, do you?"

Apparently Mr. Kaplan did. "I'm tryink to make mine gasts fillink at home."

Mr. Bloom's mocking laugh boomed across the room. "Kaplan means 'Hang your *things* in reception

hall!' " The startled look which leaped into Mr.
Kaplan's eyes showed that Norman Bloom had hit
upon the very word which he had meant to use. "But
'hang yoursalf'? Kaplan is som host!"

The gaiety was unconfined.

Suddenly a sedulous look shot into Mr. Kaplan's
eyes. He smiled. He rested his gaze first on Mrs.
Moskowitz, then on Miss Mitnick, and then—his
eyes dancing with meaning—on Norman Bloom. The
noises vanished into an expectant silence.

"Maybe isn't 'Heng your*salf* in resaption hall'
altogadder a mistake," Mr. Kaplan murmured
dreamily. "If *som* pipple came to mine house dat
vould maybe be *exactel* vat I should say."

With ten minutes left after the exercise on
idioms was completed, Mr. Parkhill put the class
through a vigorous written spelling drill. (Spelling
drills served admirably as "fillers.") He noticed that
Mr. Kaplan did not seem to be participating in the
exercise with his customary enthusiasm. Mr. Kaplan
might just as well have been in a telephone booth:
he was scratching little patterns, aimlessly, on a page
torn out of his notebook.

"Restaurant." Mr. Parkhill called.

Mr. Kaplan seemed to have retired to some reverie of thought. The shame of those three sentences burned in Mr. Kaplan's soul.

"Carpenter."

Mr. Kaplan smiled, of a sudden, and began writing. His smile was lofty, supernal, with the quality of a private pleasure in some precious joke. Mr. Parkhill announced the next word as if it were a reprimand. "Confess!"

The final bell rang. The students handed in their papers and the room became a jumble of "Goodnights." Mr. Kaplan's farewell was almost lighthearted.

Mr. Parkhill took his attendance report to Miss Schnepfe, in the Principal's office, and started home. On the subway train he started to correct the spelling exercises. (Mr. Parkhill had a remarkable capacity for concentration.) Miss Mitnick had done very well, as usual. Mr. Bloom had managed to get an 80, his average mark. Mr. Scymzak had misspelled only six out of fifteen words—a splendid performance for Mr. Scymzak. Mrs. Moskowitz was still confusing English with some other, unrevealed language.

Mr. Parkhill frowned when he saw that the next paper was blank. Some student had made a mistake, handing in an empty page instead of his spelling

drill. Mr. Parkhill turned the page over, to see if
there was some mark of identification. He beheld a
bizarre conglomeration of words, designs, figures,
and strange drawings. There was an unfinished ear
and a distinct four of spades. All these were executed
in crayons of a gaudy variety.

Mr. Parkhill wrote a sentence on the page, "Mr.
Kaplan: Please submit your spelling drill next time!"
He was about to pass on to the next paper when
something caught his eye. The scribbled words that
were almost lost in the hieroglyphics seemed to *say*
something. The writing appeared to be—it was!—
poetry. Mr. Parkhill adjusted his glasses and read
what some unknown Muse, in secret visitation, had
whispered to Hyman Kaplan.

> Critsising Mitnick
> Is a picnick.
>
> Bloom, Bloom,
> Go out the room!
>
> Mrs. Moskowitz.
> By her it doesnt fits
> A dress—Size 44.

It was a terrible vengeance which Mr. Kaplan,
mighty even in defeat, had wreaked upon those who
had tried to cast dishonor on his name.

MR. K*A*P*L*A*N'S
DARK LOGIC

FOR a long time Mr. Parkhill had believed that the incredible things which Mr. Hyman Kaplan did to the English language were the products of a sublime and transcendental ignorance. That was the only way, for example, that he could account for Mr. Kaplan's version of the name of the fourth President of the United States: "James Medicine." Then Mr. Parkhill began to feel that it wasn't ignorance which governed Mr. Kaplan so much as *impulsiveness*. That would explain the sentence Mr. Kaplan had given in vocabulary drill, using the word "orchard": "Each day he is giving her a dozen orchards." But then came Mr. Kaplan's impetuous answer to the question: "And what is the opposite of 'rich'?"

"Skinny!" Mr. Kaplan had cried.

Now a less conscientious teacher might have dismissed that as a fantastic guess. But Mr. Parkhill thought it over with great care. (Mr. Parkhill stopped at nothing in his pedagogical labors.) And he realized that to Mr. Kaplan wealth and avoirdupois were inseparable aspects of one natural whole: rich people were fat. Grant this major premise and the opposite of "rich" *must* be—it was all too clear —"skinny."

The more Mr. Parkhill thought this over the more was he convinced that it was neither ignorance nor caprice which guided Mr. Kaplan's life and language. It was Logic. A secret kind of logic, perhaps. A private logic. A dark and baffling logic. But Logic. And when Mr. Kaplan fell into grammatical error, it was simply because his logic and the logic of the world did not happen to coincide. Mr. Parkhill came to suspect that on such occasions there was only one defensible position to take: *de gustibus non est disputandum.*

Any final doubts Mr. Parkhill might have felt on the whole matter were resolved once and for all when Mr. Kaplan conjugated "to die" as "die, dead, funeral."

It was on a Monday night, several weeks after Mr. Kaplan's incomparable analysis of "to die," that Mr. Parkhill was given a fresh glimpse of the dialectical genius of his most remarkable student. The class was making three-minute addresses. Miss Rochelle Goldberg was reciting. She was describing her experience with a ferocious dog. The dog's name, according to Miss Goldberg, was "Spots." He was a "Scotch Terror."

"Was he a beeg, wild dug!" Miss Goldberg said, her eyes moving in recollective fear. "Honist, you would all be afraid somthing tarrible! I had good rizzon for being all scared. I was trying to pat Spots, nize, on the had, and saying, 'Here, Spots, Spots, Spots!'—and Spots bite me so hod on the—"

" 'Bite' is the *present* tense, Miss Goldberg."

A look of dismay wandered into Miss Goldberg's eyes.

"You want the—er—*past* tense." Mr. Parkhill spoke as gently as he could: Miss Goldberg had a collapsible nervous system. "What *is* the past tense of 'to bite'?"

Miss Goldberg hung her head.

"The past tense of 'to bite'—anyone?"

Mr. Kaplan's Samaritan impulses surged to the fore. "Isn't 'bited,' ufcawss," he ventured archly.

"No, it isn't—er—'bited'!" Mr. Parkhill couldn't tell whether Mr. Kaplan had uttered a confident negation or an oblique question.

Miss Mitnick raised her hand, just high enough to be recognized. " 'Bit,' " she volunteered, quietly. "Good, Miss Mitnick! 'Bite, *bit*, bitten.' "

At once Mr. Kaplan closed his eyes, cocked his head to one side, and began whispering to himself. "Mitnick gives 'bit' . . . *'Bit'* Mitnick gives . . . My!"

This dramaturgic process indicated that Mr. Kaplan was subjecting Miss Mitnick's contribution to his most rigorous analysis. Considering the ancient and acrid feud between these two, to allow one of Miss Mitnick's offerings to go unchallenged would constitute a psychological defeat of no mean proportions to Mr. Kaplan. It would be a blow to his self-respect. It would bring anguish to his soul.

" 'Bite, *bit*, bitten?' . . . Hmmmm . . . Dat sonds awful fonny! . . ."

It was no use for Mr. Parkhill to pretend that he had not heard: the whole class had heard.

"Er—isn't that clear, Mr. Kaplan?"

Mr. Kaplan did not open his eyes. "*Clear*, Mr. Pockheel? Foist-cless clear! Clear like gold! Only I. don' see *vy* should be dat 'bit.' . . . It don' makink *sanse!*"

"Oh, it doesn't make *sense*." Mr. Parkhill repeated lamely. Suddenly he glimpsed a golden opportunity. "You mean it isn't—er—*logical?*"

"Exactel!" cried Mr. Kaplan happily. "Dat 'bit' isn't logical."

"Well, Mr. Kaplan. Surely you remember our verb drills. The verb 'to bite' is much like, say, the verb 'to hide.' 'To hide' is conjugated 'hide, hid, hidden.' Why, then, isn't it—er—logical that the principal parts of 'to bite' be 'bite, bit, bitten'?"

Mr. Kaplan considered this semi-syllogism in silence. Then he spoke. "*I* tought de pest time 'bite' should be—'bote.'"

Miss Mitnick gave a little gasp.

"'Bote?'" Mr. Parkhill asked in amazement. "'Bote?'"

"'Bote!'" said Mr. Kaplan.

Mr. Parkhill shook his head. "I don't see your point."

"Vell," sighed Mr. Kaplan, with a modest shrug, "if is 'write, wrote, written' so vy isn't 'bite, bote, bitten'?"

Psychic cymbals crashed in Mr. Parkhill's ears.

"There is not such a word 'bote,'" protested Miss Mitnick, who took this all as a personal affront. Her voice was small, but desperate.

" 'Not-soch-a-void!' " Mr. Kaplan repeated iron-
ically. "Mine dear Mitnick, don' *I* know is not soch
a void? Did I said *is* soch a void? All I'm eskink is,
isn't logical *should be* soch a void!"

The silence was staggering.

"Mr. Kaplan, there is *no such word*, as Miss Mitnick just said." (Miss Mitnick was in agony, biting
her lips, twisting her handkerchief, gazing with bewilderment at her shoes. Her plight was that of common humanity, faced by genius.) "Nor is it—er—
logical that there *should* be such a word." Mr. Parkhill recapitulated the exercise on regular and irreg-
ular verbs. He gave the principal parts of a dozen
samples. He analyzed the whole system of verb
conjugation. Mr. Parkhill spoke with earnestness
and rare feeling. He spoke as if a good deal depended
on it.

By the time Mr. Parkhill had finished his little
lecture, Mr. Kaplan had seen the light and submitted, with many a sigh, to the tyranny of the ir-
regular verb; Miss Mitnick's normal pallor had returned; Mrs. Moskowitz was fast asleep; and Miss
Goldberg, completely forgotten in the clash between
two systems of thought, had taken her seat with the
air of one washing her hands of the whole business.

Recitation and Speech went on.

Mr. Sam Pinsky delivered a short address on the mysteries of his craft, baking. (It came out that Mr. Pinsky had produced literally thousands of "loafers" of "brat" in his career.) Miss Valuskas described a wedding she had recently attended. Mrs. Moskowitz, refreshed by her slumbers, indulged in a moving idyll about a trip she was hoping to make, to a metropolis called "Spittsburgh." Then the recess bell rang.

The second student to recite after the recess was Hyman Kaplan. He hurried to the front of the room, glowing with joy at the opportunity to recite. He almost seemed to give off a radiance.

"Ladies an' gantleman, Mr. Pockheel," Mr. Kaplan began, with customary éclat. "Tonight, I'll gonna talkink abot noose-peppers, dose movvellous—"

"Pardon me." Mr. Parkhill knew it would be nothing short of fatal to give Mr. Kaplan free rein. "It's 'Tonight I *am going* . . . to *talk.*' And the word is '*New*spapers,' not 'noose-peppers.' " Mr. Parkhill went to the board and printed "NOOSE," "PEPPER," and "NEWSPAPER." He explained the meaning of each word. When he pointed out that "pepper" was a strong condiment ("Salt . . . pep-per, Mr. Kaplan. Do you see?"), everyone smiled. Miss Mitnick rejoiced. Mr. Kaplan beamed. Mr. Kaplan was amazed by the ingenious combination ("noose-pepper") which he had brought into being.

"Vell," Mr. Kaplan took up his tale after Mr. Parkhill was done, "de *news-pa*pers is to me de finest kind ting ve have in tsivilization. Vat *is* a newspaper? Ha! It's a show! It's a comedy! It's aducation! It's movvellous!" Rhapsodically, Mr. Kaplan painted the glory and the miracle of journalism. "Fromm newspapers de messes gat—"

" 'M*a*sses,' Mr. Kaplan, 'm*a*sses'!" Mr. Parkhill felt that "messes" might have consequences too dreadful to contemplate.

"—de m*a*sses loin abot de voild. Even de edvoi-tismants in de paper is a kind lasson. An' ufcawss de odder pots a newspaper: de hatlininks, de auditorials, de cottoons, de fine pages pictchiss on Sonday, dat ve callink rotogravy sactions."

" 'Rotogra*vure!*' "

"An' in newspapers ve find ot all dat's heppenink all hover de voild! Abot politic, crimes, all kinds dif-ference *scendels* pipple makink, abot if is goink to be

snow or rainink, an' ufcawss—'spacially in U. S.—
all abot Sax!"

Mr. Parkhill closed his eyes.

"Mitout newspapers vat vould ve humans be?"
Mr. Kaplan paused dramatically. "Ha! *Sawages* ve
vould be, dat's vat! *Ignorance* ve vould fill, dat's all.
No fects! No knolledge! No aducation!" A shudder
passed through the body scholastic at the mere
thought of such a barbaric state.

"Vell, dis mornink I vas readink a noos—a *news*-
paper. English newspaper!" Mr. Kaplan paused,
awaiting the acclaim of his colleagues. They were
inert. "*English* newspaper I vas readink!" Mr. Kaplan repeated delicately. Mr. Bloom snickered, ever
the skeptic. Mr. Kaplan shot him a look composed
of indignation, pain, and ice. "I vas readink abot how
vill maybe be annodder Voild Var. So vat de paper
said? Vell, he said dat—"

"Mr. Kaplan," Mr. Parkhill *had* to interpolate.
"It's '*it* said,' not '*he* said'!"

Mr. Kaplan was stunned. "Not 'he'?"

"No, not 'he.' 'It!' Er—you know the rules for
pronouns, Mr. Kaplan. 'He' is masculine, 'she' is
feminine. Sometimes, of course, we say 'she' for cer-

tain objects which have no sex—a country, for example, or a ship. But for newspapers we use the neuter pronoun." Mr. Parkhill had an inspiration. "Surely *that's* logical!"

Mr. Kaplan sank into mighty thought, shaking his head at regular intervals. He whispered to himself: "Not mascoolin . . . Not faminine . . . But *in de meedle!*"

Mr. Parkhill waited with the patience of his calling.

"Aha!" Some cosmic verity had groped its way into Mr. Kaplan's universe. "Plizz, Mr. Pockheel. I unnistand *fine* abot mascoolin, faminine, an' neutral; but—"

" 'Neu*ter*,' Mr. Kaplan!"

"—an' neu*ter*. But is maybe all right ve should say 'he' abot *som* papers? Ven dey havink mascoolin *names?*"

Mr. Parkhill frowned. "I don't see what the name of the paper has to do with it. We say of the New York *Times*, for instance, 'it said.' Or of the New York *Post*—"

"*Dose* papers, yassir!" Mr. Kaplan cried. "But ven a paper got a real *mascoolin* name?"

Mr. Parkhill spoke with calculated deliberation.
"I don't understand, Mr. Kaplan. Which newspaper
would you say has a—er—*masculine* name?"

Mr. Kaplan's face was drenched with modesty.
"*Harold Tribune*," he said.

MR. K*A*P*L*A*N
CUTS A GORDIAN KNOT

"TONIGHT," Mr. Parkhill said, "we shall devote the entire period to our—er—examination."

It was not really necessary for Mr. Parkhill to go through the formality of an examination. He knew, many weeks before the end of the year, which of the students in the beginners' grade deserved to be promoted to Miss Higby's Composition, Grammar, and Civics, and which students, by any measure of skill, would have to be held back. Miss Mitnick, for example, was unquestionably the best student in the class. There was no doubt about her right to promotion. Or that of Mr. Feigenbaum, who had submitted some of the best compositions. At the other extreme there were students like Mrs. Moskowitz. By no stretch of the pedagogical imagination could poor Mrs. Moskowitz be considered ready for Miss Higby. Nor could Mr. Hyman Kaplan.

Mr. Parkhill frowned as he thought of Mr. Kaplan. Mr. Kaplan was certainly his most energetic and

ebullient pupil. He never missed a lesson; he never
grew discouraged; the smile of undaunted hope and
good-will never left his cherubic face. But, unfortu-
nately, Mr. Kaplan never seemed to *learn* anything.
His spelling remained erratic, his grammar deplor-
able, his sentence structure fantastic. There was only
one word for Mr. Kaplan's idioms—atrocious. As for
Mr. Kaplan's speech, if anything it grew more
astounding from day to day. Only last week Mr.
Kaplan had announced that his wife suffered "fromm
high blood pleasure." And in a drill on adjectives
he had given the positive, comparative, and superlative forms of "cold" as "cold, colder, below zero."
Mr. Parkhill often wondered whether there wasn't
something sacrilegious in trying to impose the iron
mold of English on so unfettered an intelligence.

Mr. Parkhill could go right through the class list
that way, picking the promotion-worthy from the
promotion-unworthy. He needed no examination to
aid him in the task. But Mr. Parkhill realized that
examinations lent a certain dignity and prestige to
the American Night Preparatory School for Adults.
They had a valuable *psychological* effect. And this
was the night for which the examination had been
announced.

"Please clear the arms of your chairs of everything except paper. Keep plenty of paper, please, and pens or pencils."

Smiles, frowns, and grins appeared on the faces of the students, according to their individual expectations.

"How's abot holdink bladders?" asked Mr. Kaplan.

"*Blotters*, Mr. Kaplan! Er—yes, you may keep blotters. Is everyone ready?"

Eyes alert, hearts pounding nervously, pens and pencils poised like falcons, the beginners' grade awaited the fateful event of examination. In the eyes of some students there were already visions of Composition, Grammar, and Civics, and Miss Higby.

"The first part of the examination will be a combined spelling-vocabulary test," said Mr. Parkhill. "Write a short sentence with each of the words I shall call off. Underline the word used. Is that clear to everyone?"

From the agonized expression on Mrs. Moskowitz's face it was *too* clear.

"Very well, '*knees.*'" Mr. Parkhill waited a moment and repeated, "'*Knees!*'" being careful to pronounce it as distinctly as possible: "*Neez.*"

The class attacked "knees." Mr. Kaplan promptly leaned his head back, closed his eyes, and held solemn communion with himself. This was done by whispering, in a semi-public tone, " 'Neez.' . . . 'Neez.' . . . A fonny void. . . . So be careful. . . . 'Neez.' . . . Aha! Has *two* minninks. . . . Vun, a pot mine lag. . . . Also? . . . Aha! Mine brodder's daughter is mine nee—"

"Mr. Kaplan!" Mr. Parkhill was dismayed. "*Please.* You must not—er—disturb the class."

"I back you podden," murmured Mr. Kaplan with an injured air. Mr. Kaplan could think clearly *only* by whispering to himself, as if consulting a more rational self. Mr. Parkhill's edict, however much designed to preserve the peace of the classroom, was tantamount to an intellectual death sentence for Hyman Kaplan. It strangled cerebration at its very source. Mr. Kaplan shook his head sadly, marvelling at the inhumanity of man to man.

" 'Heat,' " said Mr. Parkhill, not daring to meet Mr. Kaplan's melancholy gaze. " 'Heat!' "

" 'Heat,' " whispered Mr. Kaplan automatically, and with uncharacteristic feebleness. Then he caught himself, pressed his lips together resolutely, and

wrote in silence. He looked pale. He seemed to grow
paler and paler as he maintained the silence.

"'Pack.' . . . 'Excite.' . . . 'Throat.' "

Spelling-vocabulary continued on its even course.
Mr. Parkhill announced the words slowly, allowing
as much as three minutes for a word; he articulated
each word with laudible precision. ("Excite" he repeated no less than four times.) So well did he time
himself that he called the last of the twenty words
on his list, "Adorable," just as the recess bell rang.
The first part of the examination was over. A wave
of relief swept through the class, like a sweet summer
breeze. The students handed in their papers and
swarmed into the corridors to relax from the gruel-
ling ordeal.

Mr. Parkhill began to sort the papers. He noticed
that Miss Mitnick had, as usual, done excellently.
Mrs. Friedman seemed to have struck disaster with
"Throat." She had written several sentences,
scratched them out, and left: "He *throat* the ball real
fast." When Mr. Parkhill came to the paper headed
"H * Y * M * A * N   K * A * P * L * A * N," he sighed
automatically. He read the sentences which Mr. Kaplan had contributed to knowledge.

1. My brother Maxs' little girl (I am Uncle) is my *neece.*
2. I *heat* him on the head, the big fool.
3. I am buyink a fine *peck* potatoes.
4. In a theatre is the Insite, the Outsite and the *Exite.* (for Fire).

Then Mr. Parkhill read no more.

At 8:40 the bell rang again, ending the recess, and the students returned to their purgatory. They looked serious, a trifle worried, and tense. Mr. Parkhill, the cadences of Mr. Kaplan's bizarre sentences still ringing in his ears, *felt* serious, a trifle worried, and tense.

Mrs. Moskowitz and Mr. Kaplan entered side by side. Mr. Kaplan beamed with some inner joy. He seemed to have forgiven and forgotten the heartless edict against his whispering. Mrs. Moskowitz was moaning, as if in pain.

"I'm shaking insite, Mr. Kaplan," she said.

Mr. Kaplan raised his head with a gallant flourish. "*Stop* shakink insite!" he cried. "Lissen, Moskovitz. Kipp high de had! Kipp couratch! Dis pot haxemination vill be a tsinch, a *snep.* Dat's all, a *snep.*"

Mrs. Moskowitz took a deep sigh, admiring Mr. Kaplan's morale. "I vish I had your noives, honist." Mr. Kaplan accepted this tribute with a gracious nod. "I'll *halp* you mit de haxemination," he confided in a megaphonic whisper. "An' ven you fillink blue, remamber de song dey sinking in U. S.: 'Heppy Dace Is Here Vunce More!' " Mr. Kaplan hummed a few bars of that classic ballad to lend weight to his counsel. "Vill give you strangt! 'Heppy Dace *Is* Here Vunce More!' "

Mr. Parkhill rapped his pencil on the desk at this point, interrupting an immortal conversation. Mr. Kaplan nodded encouragement to Mrs. Moskowitz again, sat down in his chair, and cried a last buoyant word across the room. "Don' give op de sheep, Moskovitz!" It was like a call to the colors.

Mr. Parkhill explained the second part of the examination. "A one-page composition," he said firmly. "On any subject."

Several fallen faces testified to the magnitude of this assignment.

"Please do *not* talk during this part of the examination. I shall not be able to answer any questions, so please do not ask them. And do not—er—try to get help from your neighbors." Mr. Parkhill sent a searching look in the general direction of Mr. Kaplan. Mr. Kaplan nodded loyally, and then shrugged his shoulders toward Mrs. Moskowitz. Mrs. Moskowitz looked as if the last psychic leg had been cut from under her. "I suggest you begin at once. You will have the rest of the period for the composition."

Silence fell like a pall upon the beginners' grade. The wheels of creative imagination began to turn— rather slowly. Miss Caravello stared at the lithograph of George Washington on the wall, seeking inspiration, somehow, from that heroic visage. Mr. George Weinstein placed a hand over both eyes, signifying concentration. Mrs. Rodriguez yawned. Mr. Parkhill felt that "A Composition—Any Subject" would prove a decided success.

He waited a little while for the students to adjust themselves to their new problem, then sauntered down the aisle to see how the compositions were progressing. All the students were hard at work, grimacing through the opening paragraphs of their prose —all except Mrs. Moskowitz. She sat with a dumb, bewildered look. There was anguish in her eyes. Little beads of sweat on her upper lip proclaimed the effort of thought.

"Is anything wrong, Mrs. Moskowitz?" whispered Mr. Parkhill anxiously.

Mrs. Moskowitz raised a haggard face. "I ken't tink of a sobject!"

"Oh," murmured Mr. Parkhill. "Er—why not try 'My Ambition'?" "My Ambition" was a *very* popular topic.

Mrs. Moskowitz shook her head. Apparently Mrs. Moskowitz had no particular ambition.

"Er—how about 'My First Day in America'?"

"I'm sick of telling about dat," sighed Mrs. Moskowitz.

"I see," said Mr. Parkhill miserably. It was a desperate situation.

Suddenly a gentle whistle soared through the air. It was soft, but it had a haunting vibrance. Everyone looked up. The whistle caressed the lilting refrain of "Heppy Dace Is Here Vunce More."

"Mr. Kap—"

A disembodied whisper rose from the front row. "Sobjecks for composition . . . 'Should Ladies Smoke?' . . . 'Is Dere a God, Ectual?' . . . Tink abot a *qvastion*."

"Mr. Kaplan!" said Mr. Parkhill severely.

But the mysterious process of communication had been consummated. A light shone in Mrs. Moskowitz's eyes. "I'll write about a *quastion*," she said.

Mr. Parkhill moved on. He felt quite helpless. He wondered how Mr. Kaplan had heard the colloquy between him and Mrs. Moskowitz. He wondered whether Mr. Kaplan had some sort of hyperaesthesia of the ears. So entranced was he by this fancy that he did not notice that Mr. Kaplan had, for some strange reason, risen.

"Podden me, Mr. Pockheel—"

Mr. Parkhill shook his head at once. This was going too far. "I can*not* answer any questions, Mr. Kaplan."

Mr. Kaplan nodded humbly. "Is no qvastion," he said softly. "Is awful hot in de room, so maybe I should haupen op a vindow."

Mr. Kaplan "haupened op" a window.

Five minutes after Mr. Kaplan had returned to his seat, Miss Rochelle Goldberg, on his left, began to whisper something to him.

Mr. Parkhill cleared his throat in patent reprimand.

Mr. Kaplan stood up again. "I must close *don* de vindow," he sighed. "Is on Goldboig's feet a tarrible graft."

He was "closing don" the window before Mr. Parkhill could say, "*D*raft, Mr. Kaplan, *d*raft."

It was with relief that Mr. Parkhill began to arrange the composition papers in a pile after the final bell had rung and the students were gone. The titles at the tops of the pages paraded before him. "My Friend's New House." "A Sad Night in Hospitel." "Should Be Dad Panelty for Murdering?" (That looked like an unmistakable Kaplan title; no, it was Mrs. Moskowitz's paper, but it showed Mr. Kaplan's advisory influence all too clearly.) "My 4 Children Make Me a Happy Life." "Liberty Stateu." "Thinking About."

Mr. Parkhill started. He read the title again. There it was, in bold letters: "Thinking About." Mr. Parkhill raised the sheet a little above the rest of the pile.

"Thinking About"
(Humans & Enimals)

Mr. Parkhill took a deep breath and raised the page a little higher yet.

by

H * Y * M * A * N   K * A * P * L * A * N

Before he had weighed the full consequences of his folly, Mr. Parkhill was reading the composition graced by so provocative a title:

1.

Somtime I feel sad about how som people are living. Only sleeping eating working in shop. Not *thinking*. They are just like Enimals the same, which dont thinking also. Humans should not be like Enimals! They should *Thinking!* This is with me a deep idea.

Now we are having in school the axemination—a Comp. Mostly, will the students write a *story* for Comp. But I am asking, Why must allways be a story? Mr. P. must be sick and tierd from storys. Kaplan, be a man! No story! Tell better about *Thinking* somthing! Fine. Now I am thinking.

2.

In the recass was som students asking if is right to say Its Me or Its I—(because maybe we will have that question in axemination). Its Me or Its I—a planty hard question, no? Yes.

But it isnt so hard if we are *thinking about!* I figgure in this way:

If sombody is in hall besides my door, and makes knok, knok, knok; so I holler netcheral "Whose there"? Comes the anser "Its Me." A fine anser!! Who is that Me anyho? Can I tell? No! So is Its Me no good.

Again is knok, knok, knok. And again I holler "Whose there"? Now comes the anser "Its I." So who is now that I?? Still can I (Kaplan) tell?? Ha! Umpossible! So is Its I rotten also.

So it looks like is no anser. (Turn around paige)

As Mr. Parkhill turned the page "around" (Mr. Kaplan had interpreted "a one-page composition" with characteristic generosity), he could see how, put that way, the problem of "Its Me" or "Its I" was a very Gordian knot.

But must be *som kind anser.* So how we can find him out??? BY THINKING ABOUT. (Now I show how Humans isnt Enimals)

3.

If *I* am in hall and make knok, knok, knok; and I hear insite (insite the room) sombody hollers "Whose there"?—I anser strong *"Its Kaplan!"!!*

Now is fine! Plain, clear like gold, no chance mixing up Me, I, Ect.

By *Thinking* is Humans making big edvences on Enimals. This we call Progriss.

T-H-E E-N-D

Only after he had read the composition twice did
Mr. Parkhill notice that there was a postscript to
this expedition into the realm of pure logic. It was
like the signature to a masterpiece.

ps. I dont care if I dont pass, I *love* the class.